U.S. NAVAL

Chronicles

For nearly a century and a half since a group of concerned naval officers gathered to provide a forum for the exchange of constructive ideas, the U.S. Naval Institute has been a unique source of information relevant to the nation's sea services. Through the open forum provided by *Proceedings* and *Naval History* magazines, Naval Institute Press (the book-publishing arm of the institute), a robust Oral History program, and more recent immersion in various cyber activities (including the *Naval Institute Blog* and *Naval Institute News*), USNI has built a vast assemblage of intellectual content that has long supported the Navy, Marine Corps, and Coast Guard as well as the nation as a whole.

Recognizing the potential value of this exceptional collection, USNI has embarked on a number of new platforms to reintroduce readers to significant portions of this virtual treasure trove. The U.S. Naval Institute Chronicles series focuses on the relevance of history by resurrecting appropriate selections that are built around various themes, such as battles, personalities, and service components. Available in both paper and eBook versions, these carefully selected volumes help readers navigate through this intellectual labyrinth by providing some of the best contributions that have provided unique perspectives and helped shape naval thinking over the many decades since the institute's founding in 1873.

The U.S. Naval Institute on
VIETNAM
COASTAL AND RIVERINE WARFARE

THE U.S. NAVAL INSTITUTE ON

VIETNAM
COASTAL AND RIVERINE WARFARE

THOMAS J. CUTLER
SERIES EDITOR

Naval Institute Press
Annapolis, Maryland

Naval Institute Press
291 Wood Road
Annapolis, MD 21402

Library of Congress Cataloging-in-Publication Data
Names: Cutler, Thomas J., 1947–, editor of compilation. | United States Naval
    Institute, issuing body.
Title: The U.S. Naval Institute on Vietnam : coastal and riverine warfare /
    Thomas J. Cutler.
Other titles: U.S. Naval Institute on Vietnam, coastal and riverine warfare
Description: Annapolis, Maryland : Naval Institute Press, [2016] | Includes index.
Identifiers: LCCN 2016005088 | ISBN 9781682470480 (alk. paper) |
    ISBN 9781682470497 (ebook)
Subjects: LCSH: Vietnam War, 1961–1975—Riverine operations, American. |
    United States. Mobile Riverine Force—Biography.
Classification: LCC DS558.7 .U48 2016 | DDC 959.704/345—dc23
    LC record available at http://lccn.loc.gov/2016005088

♾ Print editions meet the requirements of ANSI/NISO z39.48–1992
(Permanence of Paper).
Printed in the United States of America.

24 23 22 21 20 19 18 17 16   9 8 7 6 5 4 3 2 1
First printing

CONTENTS

EDITOR'S NOTE

BECAUSE THIS BOOK is an anthology, containing documents from different time periods, the selections included here are subject to varying styles and conventions. Other variables are introduced by the evolving nature of the Naval Institute's publication practices. For those reasons, certain editorial decisions were required in order to avoid introducing confusion or inconsistencies and to expedite the process of assembling these sometimes disparate pieces.

Gender
Most jarring of the differences that readers will encounter are likely those associated with gender. A number of the included selections were written when the armed forces were primarily a male domain and so adhere to purely masculine references. I have chosen to leave the original language intact in these documents for the sake of authenticity and to avoid the complications that can arise when trying to make anachronistic adjustments. So readers are asked to "translate" (converting the ubiquitous "he" to "he or she" and "his" to "her or his" as required) and, while doing so, to celebrate the progress that we have made in these matters in more recent times.

Author "Biographies"

Another problem arises when considering biographical information of the various authors whose works make up this special collection. Some of the selections included in this anthology were originally accompanied by biographical information about their authors. Others were not. Those "biographies" that do exist have been included. They pertain to the time the article was written and may vary in terms of length and depth, some amounting to a single sentence pertaining to the author's current duty station, others consisting of several paragraphs that cover the author's career.

Ranks

I have retained the ranks of the authors *at the time of their publication*. As noted above, some of the authors wrote early in their careers, and the sagacity of their earlier contributions says much about the individuals, about the significance of the Naval Institute's forum, and about the importance of writing to the naval services—something that is sometimes underappreciated.

Other Anomalies

Readers may detect some inconsistencies in editorial style, reflecting staff changes at the Naval Institute, evolving practices in publishing itself, and various other factors not always identifiable. Some of the selections will include citational support, others will not. Authors sometimes coined their own words and occasionally violated traditional style conventions. *Bottom line:* with the exception of the removal of some extraneous materials (such as section numbers from book excerpts) and the conversion to a consistent font and overall design, these articles and excerpts appear as they originally did when first published.

ACKNOWLEDGMENTS

THIS PROJECT would not be possible without the dedication and remarkable industry of Denis Clift, the Naval Institute's vice president for planning and operations and president emeritus of the National Intelligence University. This former naval officer, who served in the administrations of eleven successive U.S. presidents and was once editor in chief of *Proceedings* magazine, bridged the gap between paper and electronics by single-handedly reviewing the massive body of the Naval Institute's intellectual content to find many of the treasures included in this anthology.

A great deal is also owed to Mary Ripley, Janis Jorgensen, Rebecca Smith, Judy Heise, Debbie Smith, Elaine Davy, and Heather Lancaster who devoted many hours and much talent to the digitization project that is at the heart of these anthologies.

Introduction

IT IS PROBABLY FAIR TO SAY that most Americans do not realize that the U.S. Navy and Coast Guard served "in-country" (as opposed to serving on ships off the coast or in aircraft over North Vietnam) during the Vietnam War. Considering that U.S. service personnel topped a half-million at the height of the war, and the Navy and Coast Guard combined never exceeded 40,000 at any given time, this in-country participation is proportionally very small. Yet over the course of the war, nearly two million Sailors and Coast Guardsmen did indeed serve in South Vietnam, and did so in a wide variety of ways. Some gave their lives or their limbs in that service.

While Navy participation in the war included construction battalions (SeaBees), SEALs, advisors to the South Vietnamese navy, and some others, a significant number served in the rather iconoclastic realms of coastal and riverine warfare. Often generically lumped under the semi-descriptive sobriquet of "brown water navy," four different task forces were organized for the different missions deemed necessary during the course of the war. TF115 served as the Coastal Surveillance Force (Operation Market Time); TF116 was the River Patrol Force (Operation Game

Warden); TF117 worked with the Army as the River Assault Group (a component of the joint Mobile Riverine Force); and TF194 was formed later in the war to carry out a new strategy known as Operation SEA-LORDS. These different groups performed different but related tasks that contrasted sharply with those of the so-called "blue-water navy."

Through the years of the war and beyond, the Naval Institute has covered these operations in detail through books, articles, and oral histories. This anthology represents only a relatively small portion of that greater corpus, but has been assembled to give a reasonably comprehensive account of those unusual operations. Conspicuously absent are a number of wonderfully comprehensive articles that appeared in the specially prepared Naval Review issues and many oral histories by key players—omitted only because of their size, not their quality.

For those who served, this collection will bring back memories; for those who did not, the selections included will serve as edification and, in some cases, as inspiration, while recounting a unique chapter in the proud histories of both the Navy and Coast Guard.

"The River War in Indochina"

1

Robert McClintock

U.S. Naval Institute *Proceedings*
(December 1954): 1303–11

THE MOST IMPORTANT RIVER-WARFARE since the operations of the Federal Navy against New Orleans and Vicksburg has been carried on during the past eight years in Indochina. Even the so-called "River War" of Winston Churchill—Kitchener's campaign for upper Egypt and the Sudan—was fought largely on land and the Nile was but the artery of a logistical system. However, in Indochina the rivers of that peninsula have been the avenue of access to the battlefront and frequently the battlefront itself.

If one looks at a chart of Indochina, the importance of the river war in the fighting which recently was terminated by the ceasefire at Geneva becomes immediately apparent. There are two vast deltas; one the Delta of Tonkin which comprises the river systems of the Riviere Rouge, of the Noire, and of the Claire (picturesque and literal names, the Red, the Black, and the Clear); while in the South, in Cambodia and Cochin-China, there is the Delta of the mighty Mekong. In both Deltas the sodden rice paddy is traversed by a maze of meandering streams, connected here and there by the straightedge of a canal. During the monsoon rains the Deltas flood, and the only means of transport is by water.

Some French naval officers have gone so far as to estimate that ninety percent of the communications system of Indochina is by water, whether by the China Sea, the rivers and their confluences, or by canal. It is certain that under conditions of the recent war where land communications, both by rail and road, were severed by the Vietminh, the river systems assumed an ever more vital aspect.

Thus, as the French Vice Admiral Ortoli has pointed out in an article on the French Navy in Indochina which was published in the *Revue Maritime* in December, 1952, owing to the peculiar geography of the country the French Navy found itself fighting as far into the interior as its means would take it. Ortoli listed five principal missions of the French Navy in the war in Indochina:

1. To control the coast in order to provide freedom of access and maneuver;
2. To interdict coastal waters to the enemy;
3. To clear mines from ports and waterways;
4. To use naval aviation for patrol, precision bombing, and direct support of land and naval forces;
5. To serve in clearing and controlling the network of interior waterways which serve as the principal means of access to the life of the country.

Ortoli commented: "This network of great rivers, streams, creeks, and canals results in that maneuver, which in the military sense of the word, has the ship as its instrument of execution." Ortoli went on to comment,

"The security and the command of the waterways have fallen very naturally on the Navy; but in a country where a continuous front line does not exist, where the mutual osmosis of opposing forces is permanent, in brief, where the enemy is everywhere and nowhere, the Navy finds itself faced with an absolutely new problem.

"For after all, although the Navy has frequently been asked permanently to assure the use of threatened waterways whose banks are in friendly hands, and although the Navy has been asked temporarily, by a task force, to assure the security of waterways whose shores are in enemy hands, never yet has any navy been asked permanently to assure the security or use of waterways whose banks are hostile."

How did the French Navy come to find itself fighting the river war in Indochina?

When the Japanese occupied Indochina, the French Naval forces, like the Army and Air Force, were immobilized and throughout most of the war contented themselves with maintaining their equipment and internal order throughout the three kingdoms of Indochina. However, on March 9, 1945, the Japanese, in their death throes, attacked the French military and naval forces and destroyed them as an effective instrument. So far as the French Navy was concerned, only certain small units, as for example, armed junks such as *Audacieuse* and *Vieux-Charles* operated in a clandestine manner in the Baie d'Along. However, with the defeat of Japan and the taking over of the Indochinese peninsula by the forces of Nationalist China as far south as the 16th parallel, and by the British from Cochin-China to that drawn line, the French Navy began to recoup its strength.

The Naval Brigade Far East was established in 1945. Its first elements disembarked at Saigon on October 19, participating in the liberation of the city. This outfit, supported by naval parachutists, fought in the campaign southward in Cochin-China; and later two river flotillas were formed, made up of junks, motor sampans, and river launches which assumed the somewhat pompous name of "river cruisers," for the cleaning out of Cochin-China from Vietminh elements.

As to what this kind of operations meant, carried out by naval small craft moving up creeks and streams in the rice paddy country of the Mekong Delta, Naval Surgeon Le Breton has given this description:[1]

"Progress across rice paddies and mangrove thickets forced the men most of the time to struggle through water and mud. Frequent transshipments aboard LCVPs to cross river channels became exhausting; in fact, owing to the absence of roads, it was necessary to carry on one's back not only regular kit but also all the ammunition and weapons, such as machine guns and mortars. . . . And finally, for these drenched men, veritable hunks of ambulating mud, the leaden sun added to their torment."

Once Cochin-China had been "pacified," the northern tactical group of the Naval Brigade was brought to Tonkin to relieve withdrawing Chinese forces. With them went 10,000 troops of the 9th Colonial Infantry Division. They were embarked for the North in the old aircraft carrier *Bearn* at Cap St. Jacques on February 28, 1946, but when this force attempted to ascend the river to Haiphong, the port of Tonkin, on March 6, it was met with intense Chinese fire, and the French supporting flotilla was forced to withdraw. Later, following negotiations with the Nationalist Chinese, agreement was reached for the disembarkation on March 8 of the French Expeditionary Force on the Island of Haly near Haiphong, called significantly by the natives, the "Island of the Dead."

As the Chinese Nationalist Forces began to withdraw slowly from Tonkin, the French Expeditionary Corps with naval support replaced them. However, the Tonkin Delta was permeated by adherents of the Communist-led, bitterly anti-French and Nationalist-inspired Vietminh under the political leadership of Ho Chi Minh and the brilliant military command of General Giap. Accordingly, the hard-pressed French forces soon found themselves involved in fire fights in Haiphong on November 20, 1946, with Marines used as shock troops against the Vietminh attackers, and on December 19 Hanoi, the ancient capital of Vietnam, erupted in a bloody massacre of the French inhabitants. This was historically the outbreak of the eight-year war in Indochina, the river war in which the French Navy played its laborious and valiant part.

Although the military situation in Tonkin was precarious, the French, having secured Cochin-China, used Saigon as the base for a new river fleet.

A brilliant Catalan officer, Commander Francois Jaubert, was charged by General Leclerc to create the river squadrons. He had to start from scratch as the Japanese assault of March 9, 1945, had left everything in ruins. Jaubert sent a few officers scrounging for river craft, motors, docks, and a river naval base. He set up his headquarters in the former Saigon Yacht Club across the arroyo de l'Avalanche which lies across a narrow canal from the present Saigon zoo. Jaubert, who later died gallantly leading a naval attack on a river north of Bien Hoa not far from Saigon, graced the main hall of his headquarters with a huge statue of Buddha because he insisted on placing his flotillas under the tutelary protection of the gods of the country. Most of his little fleet was made up of former Japanese junks, river launches, and a squadron of 14 LCA's and 6 LCVP's brought by the aircraft carrier *Bearn* from Singapore. These landing craft were given the names of the "petites amies" of certain of the naval officers and were called *Doudou, Ramatou, Vahine, Sampanitre,* and *Mariniere.*

Even in this early period the French Navy operating on the interior waters of Indochina found a certain lack of comprehension on the part of the High Command which was in army hands. Thus, one naval officer wrote:[2]

"The [staff] discussions are sometimes troubled because it is difficult to make our Army comrades understand that the tides fix our timetables in an imperious fashion." As to the nature of the river fighting itself, the following description of a single action by Capitaine de Fregate de Brossard of an expedition in the Tonkin is typical.[3] He was in command of a unit called a Dinassaut, which is French naval terminology for "assault river division." These units are usually made up of landing craft supported (depending upon depth of water) by destroyer escorts or converted aviation tenders. However, in most cases, owing to the shallow depths encountered, the vicissitudes of tide and current, and the narrow channels of rivers and canals, the displacement of these vessels did not exceed that of LCI's and LCM's.

To return to the action described by Commander de Brossard, he has written that the Dinassaut under his command was charged with mounting the river Som sixty kilometers above the town of Dap-Cau in Tonkin. This was a sinuous river, with wide sand banks, reefs, and especially very strong barricades of bamboo placed like stockades in the main channel.

The Dinassaut unit, led by an LCI and followed by three LCM's and three LCVP's, carried troops to assault a Vietminh-held town. "The river banks, at first thronged by cheering Vietnamese, fell silent as the expedition chugged upstream into enemy country," wrote Commander de Brossard. "On the river where no one is to be seen it is impossible to eliminate the impression of hostility which seizes you." The expedition passed silent villages and noted the positions of mortar and machine gun emplacements which were waiting for their return. Farther upriver the Dinassaut had to leave the LCI because of her draft and length. A bamboo barrage was forced, after first firing at it with hedgehogs, and finally the three LCM's disembarked their infantry.

Objective accomplished, the worst was yet to come. The Dinassaut flotilla regrouped and began to descend the river. The commander, when passing a crenelated dike high above the stream, saw Vietminh troops aiming bazookas at his ship. The captain in person took over the starboard 20 mm. gun and hit one bazooka point-blank. However, general fire opened on both sides, the Vietminh pouring bazooka and machine gun fire from either high bank down onto the decks of the ships. There were heavy casualties among the crews serving the 40 mm. and 20 mm. guns. The Dinassaut had to run the gauntlet of murderous fire for seven kilometers downstream with every man on board firing back except the helmsman and the men in the engine spaces. The Dinassaut had been engaged by an entire Vietminh battalion. The action lasted half an hour. That night de Brossard landed his wounded at Dap-Cau to be taken to hospitals at Hanoi.

In addition to the constant danger of ambush and close-in fire from bazookas, mortars, and machine guns, probably the greatest danger run by the French Navy in the river war in Indochina came from mines. Although most of these were fairly crude, homemade affairs, they were exceedingly effective because they were sunk deep in the mud of the meandering streams and canals and thus almost defied sweeping. Since the majority of the Vietminh mines were controlled from hidden firing stations on the shore, they did not require antennae or other means of contact with ships passing over them and this made the problem of sweeping all the more difficult. The French Navy endeavored by using heavy wire drags to burrow into the mud of the bottom and this technique met with partial success. However, up to the day of the final cease-fire, the Navy had not yet solved the problem of the visually controlled river mine. The antidote, no doubt, was to be found in naval aviation. In those cases where the French Navy was able to fly reconnaissance ahead of Dinassaut river flotillas, aviators were able at times to locate not only the camouflaged fire control points which controlled the river mines but also the ambushes around the bends of rivers. An account of naval losses during a typical period in 1954 from the 5th of January to the 16th of February lists 14 casualties to naval craft in operations on interior waters in Indochina. It will be seen that mines, automatic weapons and bazookas were the arms of choice of the Vietminh, but there is no doubt that in respect of danger to ships the mine was the most dangerous weapon to be encountered in this fluvial campaign. Personnel suffered largely from bazooka fire and mortars. The use of flame throwers against close-in ambush was advocated by the French naval command, but not really tried on any scale before the war ended.

Nevertheless, despite the casualties suffered, the arduous nature of the climate and the ever-present enemy in this civil as well as international war, the French river fleet assumed an increasingly important role as the Indochina war drew to its conclusion. The large logistic requirements imposed by the battle of Dien Bien Phu were impeded by successful Vietminh attacks on the main line of communications from the port of Haiphong to Hanoi, the headquarters of General Cogny, who was supporting General de Castries at Dien Bien Phu. Train and truck convoys were daily blown up by land mines and thus the river and canal route between Haiphong and Hanoi became the jugular vein for the supply of Dien Bien Phu and the northern capital, Hanoi. The French Navy met this challenge with characteristic disregard of danger but took heavy losses in the process from bazooka fire in ambush and, as indicated above, from the ever-present and deadly shore controlled mines.

The war for Indochina was militarily lost at Dien Bien Phu through tactical misjudgment. The war was never at a posture where the impact of naval power would prove decisive. It was fundamentally a land war and, above all, a guerrilla war. But it was also a war in the mud, the flooded Deltas, the rivers of endless ambuscade. The French Navy met the requirements of this type of conflict in admirable fashion, adopting its techniques and use of naval craft to action across rice paddies and through the mangrove swamps of Cochin-China. That the war was not won is no reflection upon the French Navy. Its annals will imperishably list the valiant efforts of the Dinassauts, the river flotillas, and the little ships with the amorous names.

Notes
1. E. Le Breton: "Les Fusiliers Marins en Indochine"; *La Revue Maritime*, October, 1948, No. 30.
2. Capitaine de Frégate Guy Hebert: "La Naissance d'une Flotille"; *La Revue Maritime*, October, 1949, No. 42.
3. Capitaine de Frégate Brossard: "Dinassaut"; *La Revue Maritime*, January, 1953, No. 81.

For more than two decades an officer of the American Foreign Service, **Mr. McClintock** has recently been named United States Ambassador to Cambodia. During World War II he was Charge d'Affaires at Helsinki and returned to Washington to serve four years as Special Assistant to the Director of the Office of United Nations Affairs. Following that tour he served as First Secretary of the American Embassy at Brussels, as a member of the staff of the National War College, and as Charge d'Affaires of the American Embassy, Saigon, Vietnam. Mr. McClintock was the winner of the U.S. Naval Institute Prize Essay Contest in 1941.

2 "From Blue to Green and Brown"

Lieutenant Commander Thomas J. Cutler, USN (Ret.)

Naval History (December 2015): 26–34

ON THE MORNING OF 3 MARCH 1965, a UH-1B helicopter piloted by an Army lieutenant lifted off the pad at Qui Nhon on the central coast of South Vietnam and headed south. On his right, the lieutenant could see the mountains of the Chaine Annamatique, their steep slopes covered with dark green carpets of jungle foliage, their feet immersed in the blue of the South China Sea. Just before 1030, the pilot rounded the promontory that flanked the northern side of a picturesque bay known as Vung Ro.

Because they sometimes fly in tight formations, Army helicopter pilots have a finely tuned sense of relative motion, and as he surveyed the sapphire waters of the bay below, the lieutenant sensed that something was not right. Focusing on a small, vegetation-covered island he suddenly realized that it was moving!

Swooping down for a closer look, he saw that the "island" was actually a trawler whose decks and superstructure had been camouflaged with potted trees. The pilot reported his discovery, and what would enter the history books as "the Vung Ro Incident" was under way.

What this Army lieutenant did not realize at the time was that he had triggered a sequence of events that would take elements of the U.S.

Navy away from their traditional blue-water realm and send them into the green and brown waters of South Vietnam.

Sea Change

A combination of U.S. air strikes and attacks by Vietnamese navy (VNN) vessels disabled and eventually captured the intruding ship at Vung Ro. On board were large amounts of ammunition and other supplies—many bearing labels from an assortment of communist countries—as well as numerous documents and objects that made it clear the trawler had come from North Vietnam. The long-running debate about whether the North was using the sea to supply communist forces in the South was over.

But there was also concern that VNN forces had taken nearly five days to capture the ship, and U.S. Navy advisers who participated in the operation reported many significant problems with the effectiveness of their South Vietnamese counterparts. U.S. planners concluded that this now-proven threat needed to be countered by an active American effort that would transform the U.S. Navy's in-country role from nominally advisory to openly operational. This was a momentous change that would eventually bring nearly 2 million U.S. sailors and Coast Guardsmen to serve in-country over the course of the war.

The sailors who left gray decks to serve in-country traded their white hats and combination covers for black berets and helmets, their bell bottoms and khakis for green utilities and various forms of camouflage. Five-inch guns were replaced by machine guns and grenade launchers, rudders and screws gave way to Jacuzzi pumps, and malaria and dysentery joined *mal de mer* as common afflictions.

Leaving traditional career paths to serve in Vietnam sometimes proved less than career-enhancing, and in-country life lacked some of the creature comforts found in the blue-water Navy, but there have always been "swashbucklers" in the service willing to trade a swab or a typewriter for a .50-caliber machine gun, so there were many volunteers. The preferred ratings for these operations were those with applicable skills, such as boatswains, gunner's mates, and enginemen, but many other ratings were represented, with eagerness making up for the lack of vocational skills.

Market Time

The transition from advisory roles to operational ones began with the creation of the Coastal Surveillance Force, designated as Task Force (TF) 115, whose primary mission—code-named Operation Market Time—was to interdict the flow of supplies to communist forces by conducting random searches among the throngs of junks and sampans that travelled these waters on a daily basis.

Seventeen existing 82-foot patrol boats (WPBs) were provided by the Coast Guard, but for these shallow-water operations the Navy had to rely on modifying a 50-foot aluminum craft that was being used in the Gulf of Mexico to transport crews to and from offshore drilling rigs. Officially designated as PCFs (patrol craft, fast), these converts were suitably armed with machine guns and naval mortars. Capable of 28 knots, they came to be known as "Swift Boats."

Patrols were marked by extreme contrasts. A Market Time sailor typically spent weeks roasting in the Southeast Asian sun, then found himself battling pounding seas and torrential rains during the monsoon season. While stopping and searching vessels could earn him appreciative smiles from people who understood why he was there, he more often saw the scowls of fishermen and farmers who resented the delay in getting their products to market. Although he was there to help the South Vietnamese people, he could never fully trust them, which meant that despite the tedium of his mission, he could never let his guard down.

Mostly the U.S. sailors' mission was one of deterrence—like the cop on a beat—and it could be frustrating as well as boring. Occasionally a North Vietnamese trawler attempted a run into the shore, offering the opportunity to target a clearly hostile vessel, but these were relatively rare. The business of routine searching for contraband was sometimes interrupted by delivering fire support to friendly units on shore, conducting occasional search-and-rescue missions to recover downed aviators, or providing assistance to vessels in distress.

These sailors were most vulnerable when their craft were tied up at bases ashore. The threat of attack was a constant for virtually all Americans serving in South Vietnam. They never knew when rockets or mortars might rain down, or when a sniper's bullet or a sapper's explosive might send them home early in a zippered bag.

The task at hand was enormous by any calculus. Different sources estimated the daily coastal traffic of South Vietnam ranged from 4,000 to 60,000 vessels—the discrepancy of these figures telling much about the difficulties of the mission. Measuring success was challenging since the only measurable data consisted of successful intercepts and captures, whereas the number of "misses" was entirely unknown. But postwar studies suggest that TF 115 succeeded in extensively altering the enemy's logistics, substantially reducing his ability to resupply guerrilla units by sea infiltration and forcing him to rely instead on much less efficient overland supply through Laos and Cambodia.

Game Warden

The most serious infiltration by land occurred in the southernmost part of South Vietnam, in the region known as the Mekong Delta. Geographically this area represented only one quarter of the country's land area, but demographically it comprised about half of the population. It consisted of a vast network of waterways, with a spider's web of streams and canals interconnecting four main branches of the Mekong River.

Adjacent to the Delta was the Rung Sat Special Zone (also known as the "Forest of Assassins"), a foreboding maze of waterways, swamps, mangrove tangles, and islands that the communist insurgents, or Viet Cong, had inherited from the bandits and pirates who had long dominated the region. Between the Delta and the Rung Sat was the meandering Long Tau River that provided the capital city of Saigon access to the sea.

Despite the Mekong Delta's long-standing reputation as one of the great "rice bowls" of Asia, the Viet Cong controlled much of the flow of rice to South Vietnamese markets, and the VNN was having difficulty keeping the shipping channels to Saigon open, which hampered needed commercial trade. Consequently, the U.S. Navy was called on to fix these problems, and another task force (TF 116) was created, officially called the River Patrol Force.

Once again, the Navy's blue-water parochialism left it unprepared for this new campaign, known as Operation Game Warden. The needed vessels had to be created by modifying an existing 31-foot fiberglass recreational craft. Designated PBRs (patrol boats, river) these craft were powered by a pair of diesel engines designed for a maximum speed of 30 knots (not quite realized after weapons and ammunition were added). A pair of rotatable, stern-mounted jet pumps manufactured by Jacuzzi Brothers served as both propulsion and steering, obviating the need for screws and rudders. That made them less vulnerable to the vegetation and debris that proliferated in the rivers and canals. A pair of .50-caliber machine guns were mounted forward in an open mount, and a single .50-caliber was mounted aft on a centerline pedestal and often accompanied by grenade launchers or 7.62-mm M-60 machine guns on each side.

In February 1966, Game Warden officially commenced. FT 116's missions were to interdict enemy infiltration, enforce curfews, prevent taxation of water traffic by the Viet Cong, and keep the main shipping channel into Saigon open.

Seven operating bases were set up in both the Delta and Rung Sat and were supplemented by four old LSTs (landing ships, tank) that were brought out of mothballs to be fitted as mobile floating bases. A minesweeping contingent was added that consisted of 57-foot wooden MSBs (minesweeping boats) and regularly patrolled the meandering Long Tau. "Sea Wolf" helicopters (Army hand-me-down UH-1 "Hueys" flown by Navy crews) were added and later supplemented by "Black Ponies" (Army OV-10 Bronco turboprop aircraft also flown by Navy pilots) to provide air support.

Established fleet doctrine was of little use, so these brown-water sailors had to "write the book" as they went. While trial and error is rarely preferable to reliance on established procedures (because of the "error" part, which can be costly), these neophytes learned quickly and enjoyed the autonomy and flexibility that Americans often prefer at the tactical level.

Tactics evolved that included the pairing of PBRs for most operations, with a "patrol officer" (a junior officer or senior petty officer) in charge of both boats. This allowed mutual support and permitted one boat to conduct inspections while the other "hovered" nearby watching for other dangers (such as ambushes from ashore). Searches were conducted as near as possible to midstream, with one PBR maintaining clear lines of fire to both banks, while the other conducted the inspection with weapons ready, engines running, and the inspected vessels brought alongside but never moored to the inspecting PBR. (Virtually all of these procedures were violated in the famous movie *Apocalypse Now*, as a single PBR moors to a sampan, shuts down its engines, and ultimately fails to employ weapons discipline.)

In addition to search operations, PBRs conducted nighttime ambushes, aided units under attack on shore, and supported a number of SEAL counterguerrilla operations. Tactical innovations included such things as "acoustical detection devices" (Coke cans filled with pebbles strung across a canal at night), an M-60 machine gun mounted on top of the boat's canopy (to allow firing over elevated canal banks when the tide was low), and a "flamethrower" (a hunter's bow used to shoot flaming arrows).

The enemy too developed his own tactics by taking advantage of low tides to restrict the maneuverable battle space for the PBRs, faking a medical emergency on one sampan to distract U.S. sailors from countering the movements of another, and timing ambushes to occur when the Americans were returning from a long patrol and consequently fatigued.

The early frequency of ambushes by the enemy served as credible evidence that these operations were having the desired effects. Eventually the Viet Cong were driven from the major waterways. Gone were the VC tax-collecting stations; shipping flowed through the Long Tau, and enemy contact gradually fell off until tedium replaced terror as a major morale problem.

Mobile Riverine Force

Even though Game Warden operations were solving problems on the major waterways, the land areas of the Delta remained in jeopardy. Well-ensconced enemy forces operated with too much freedom in this vital geographic area, and sending in ground forces seemed the logical solution. But the U.S. Army traveled largely on wheels and treads, and there were few roads in this region. With waterways as the highways, some sort of amphibious capability was required. The U.S. Marines would have been the logical choice, but by this time they were fully occupied in "I Corps," the northernmost quarter of South Vietnam.

The solution was to designate yet another Navy task force (TF 117)—dubbed the Riverine Assault Force—that would be combined with the Army's 2nd Brigade of the 9th Infantry Division to form the Mobile Riverine Force (MRF). Mobility was provided by a large fleet of existing landing craft that were converted into various configurations and clustered around a flotilla of larger vessels, including several LSTs that were resurrected and reconfigured for the new purpose. This "jungle green" flotilla could move about the main rivers, positioning themselves where needed to root out enemy concentrations. The soldiers lived in barracks ships during transits, then embarked in modified LCM-6s (landing craft, mechanized) for assault operations.

The LCM-6s had been significantly modified for the various needs of the assault force. The most numerous were the armored troop carriers (ATCs), also known as "Tango Boats." Of the various conversions, these

56-foot craft looked most like the original landing craft, retaining the large bow doors that could be lowered onto river or canal banks to allow rapid egress of embarked troops. They were heavily armed with an array of machine guns and grenade launchers and one 20-mm cannon. Bar armor pre-detonated enemy recoilless-rifle rounds and rocket-propelled grenades before they could penetrate the troop-filled well deck. A canvas awning over the top of the well deck protected the soldiers from the sun and light grenades. With a seven-man crew, one ATC could transport and land an Army platoon (approximately 40 men) and provide close-in fire support. The craft carried spare ammunition, food, and other supplies for the initial assault and could ferry more during extended operations.

Some ATCs were modified to accommodate a steel flight deck, in place of the canvas awning, where helicopters could actually land to evacuate wounded or perform other support duties, making them the world's smallest aircraft carriers. Others, equipped with medical-aid stations, served as diminutive hospital ships, and still others with large fuel bladders functioned as counterparts to the fleet oiler.

The most formidable craft were the monitors, which functioned as the battleships of the flotilla. Although they too were once LCM-6s, their bow doors had been removed and replaced by a rounded bow. A cluster of weapons similar to those of the ATCs was complemented by a potent 81-mm naval mortar amidships and a 40-mm cannon in a forward turret. Later versions came to Vietnam with 105-mm howitzers replacing the forward cannon. Some monitors were also equipped with flamethrowers (useful for burning away heavy vegetation as well as terrorizing enemy soldiers) and dubbed "Zippos" in recognition of the cigarette lighter that many GIs carried in those days.

The CCB (command communications boat) was similar to the monitor but carried a command-and-control console amidships in place of the mortar. These functioned as a kind of flagship, their banks of HF, VHF, and UHF radios providing commanders the means to coordinate operations.

In late 1967, assault support patrol boats (ASPB) were added to the force. The only riverine craft built from scratch for service in Vietnam, they were designed to function as a hybrid destroyer-minesweeper. At 50 feet and 28 tons, these relative latecomers were crewed by seven sailors and could provide a lot of firepower from an array of machine guns and grenade launchers as well as a stern-mounted mortar and a bow-mounted 20-mm cannon. Their reinforced hulls and chain-drag mine-countermeasures rig could clear the way for an assault, and an innovative underwater exhaust system significantly reduced engine noise (but created maintenance headaches because of their complexity).

Tactics evolved as experience begat innovation. Troops began carrying lines with snaphooks to aid in water crossing and detonating booby traps; truck tires and sandbags were placed beneath mortar baseplates to absorb the shock of firing; underwear was left behind in the barracks ships because it did not dry as rapidly as fatigues.

Periodically shifting its location, the Mobile Riverine Force anchored in various rivers and conducted a wide variety of operations in both the Delta and the Rung Sat that varied in size and complexity, many large enough to warrant special operational names such as Great Bend, Concordia, and Hop Tac.

In the early hours of the Tet Offensive in early 1968, the MRF moved around the Delta, engaging enemy forces in a series of intense battles. One took place along a three-mile stretch of the Rach Ruong tributary, where the waterway narrowed to a mere 30 yards wide. Enemy forces opened up with heavy machine guns, rockets, and recoilless-rifles, and the prepared Americans retaliated with a heavy barrage, using leveled howitzers to fire deadly "Beehive" antipersonnel rounds with devastating effect, begging comparisons to broadsides exchanged in close-quarters battles during the Age of Sail. The half-hour battle left a large number of enemy dead along the banks as the MRF forces continued down the waterway to their next engagement, a 21-hour pitched battle at My Tho.

In the weeks that followed, the soldiers and sailors of the MRF fought with little rest to preserve South Vietnam's vital "rice bowl," moving around the Delta, driving enemy forces out of and away from the critical cities, inflicting heavy casualties on the Viet Cong, who had at last come out of the proverbial woodwork and into the crosshairs of American guns.

The MRF continued operations after the Tet Offensive and, as time went on, the enemy ceded control of much of the Delta territory. But it was also clear that he was not defeated. Withdrawing deeper inland and relying on the smaller waterways in those areas, he continued to infiltrate from the nearby Cambodian sanctuary that had been allowed as a result of American concerns about widening the war.

SEALORDS

When Vice Admiral Elmo R. Zumwalt Jr. arrived in South Vietnam in the fall of 1968 to take command of the in-country naval forces, he found that the three task forces had successfully carried out their missions. But he also faced two problems that begged solutions. One was the existence of the Cambodian sanctuary, and the other was that morale was suffering because declining contact with the enemy meant that patrols were becoming mind-numbingly routine. The old strategic concept of a "fleet in being" has always suffered from this problem—existence playing an important strategic role, but inactivity breeding discontent.

It was clear that it was time for a strategic adjustment, and Zumwalt responded by creating a whole new task force—TF 194—and dubbed it SEALORDS, for Southeast Asia Lake, Ocean, River, and Delta Strategy. The idea behind this new strategy was to carry the fight to the enemy by restructuring the forces available and redefining their missions.

Swift Boats were drawn from the coasts to operate in the rivers and canals, PBRs were tasked with deeper penetrations into the smaller waterways, and various elements of the MRF were reassigned to support new penetrating and blocking missions. These newly configured forces probed deeper into the Delta hinterlands to interdict enemy movements, but more important, they were tasked with establishing a barrier near the Cambodian border to cauterize the arterial bleeding that had been suffered as a result of the existing sanctuary.

Initially this new force conducted four aggressive campaigns—Operations Search Turn, Foul Deck, Giant Slingshot, and Barrier Reef—that established an effective barrier and greatly reduced the amount of infiltration.

Engagements were so common during the Giant Slingshot operation that an acronymic shorthand was developed to speed up the reporting process: ENIFFs were enemy-initiated firefights, FRIFFs were friendly-initiated firefights, while an ENENG represented contact with the enemy in which fire had been initiated by him but not returned, and a FRENG was the converse.

ENIFFS along the Vam Co Dong were so frequent that a particular stretch of the river was called "Blood Alley." In a strange but logical twist, friendly casualties increased significantly, but so did morale among those who preferred the adrenaline-fed activity to the tedium of routine patrols.

Subsequent operations with different names but similar purposes increased the pressure on the enemy and neutralized his effectiveness in various parts of the Delta. New tactics were developed that included the employment of "waterborne guard posts"—a euphemism for ambushes—and the use of giant pontoons to establish small "advanced tactical base camps" (ATSB) in remote waterways. These were eventually extrapolated into larger, more permanent, floating bases designed to maintain control of regions previously belonging to the enemy.

The Americans and their South Vietnamese allies conducted "randomized pressure" operations in the area that took various forms, including organized sorties, emergency response operations, and routine patrols. Early resistance diminished, and gradually local villagers began to provide warnings of enemy movements and plans. It was clear that Zumwalt's strategy was succeeding.

Vietnamization and Postscript

While Zumwalt's aggressive approach injected new life into the U.S. Navy's in-country operations, the progress was made less relevant by a major change in American policy. The unpopularity of the war resulted in U.S. extrication becoming the primary strategic goal. Washington directed American military commanders in Vietnam to turn the war back over to their South Vietnamese allies under a new policy called "Vietnamization." And it was clear that "sooner" outranked "later."

For the Navy's part, Admiral Zumwalt responded to this new directive by creating a graduated, on-the-job training program that he dubbed ACTOV (Accelerated Turnover to the Vietnamese). ACTOV got under way in late 1968 and proceeded at a steady rate thereafter, putting the Navy out ahead of the other services for its part in Vietnamization. The whole process took less than a year.

It had been a strange cycle that had begun with U.S. Navy personnel arriving in South Vietnam to serve as advisers to the VNN, then shifting to full combat operations in the middle years, only to be later returned to the role of advisers at the end.

Preparing for war with the Soviet Union during the Cold War had required the building of a powerful blue-water navy in a classic blend of the traditional strategic concepts of deterrence, sea control, and forward presence. And when it came time for power projection in Vietnam, the blue-water giants were more than capable of launching strikes against the communist North. But the Navy was ill-prepared for the green- and brown-water operations needed in the South. Consequently, appropriate vessels had to be created by conversions, tactical doctrine had to be developed in the crucible of combat, and many of the sailors who went in-country had to learn skills well outside their ratings. The in-country Navy had been an aberration, a jury-rig of sorts, and ultimately it was for naught.

But it was also a triumph of American adaptability and of the Navy's traditional "can-do" spirit. Despite numerous handicaps, the needed forces not only coalesced in relatively short order but were effective in turning the tide of battle in several specific areas. Infiltration from the sea was significantly reduced by Operation Market Time, vital waterways were kept open by Operation Game Warden, and enemy forces were pushed back into the hinterlands of the Mekong Delta and the Rung Sat Special Zone by the Mobile Riverine Force. And Operation SEALORDS combined the Navy's in-country assets into an aggressive assault on those forces that continued to infiltrate from the Cambodian sanctuary.

Most of the 2,663 Navy and 7 Coast Guard personnel who died in Vietnam—and thousands more who were wounded—were casualties of these anomalous operations, but for most of the in-country sailors who survived, our service was (and remains) a source of pride. And, as the years have passed, the in-country experience has lingered as an assortment of surreal memories, occasionally resurrected by the sound of a passing helicopter, or the sight of a dripping palm frond, or the ominous rumble of distant thunder.

Sources

Thomas J. Cutler, *Brown Water, Black Berets: Coastal and Riverine Warfare, Vietnam* (Annapolis, MD: Naval Institute Press, 1988).

Edward J. Marolda, *By Sea, Air, and Land: An Illustrated History of the United States Navy and the War in Southeast Asia* (Washington DC: Government Printing Office, 1994).

Richard L. Schreadley, "The Naval War in Vietnam 1950–1970," U.S. Naval Institute *Proceedings*, vol. 97, no. 5 (May 1971).

Richard L. Schreadley, "SEA LORDS." U.S. Naval Institute *Proceedings*, vol. 96, no. 8 (August, 1970).

S. A. Swarztrauber, "River Patrol Relearned." U.S. Naval Institute *Proceedings*, vol. 96, no. 5 (May 1970).

3 "The DER in MARKET TIME"

Lieutenant Commander W. J. Moredock, USN

U.S. Naval Institute *Proceedings*
(February 1967): 136–38

WITH THE DISBANDING of the early warning barriers in the Atlantic and Pacific in mid-1965, 14 radar picket escort ships found themselves making hasty preparations to take up new patrol stations around South Vietnam. These DERs would become part of Operation MARKET TIME, the effort to halt the Communist infiltration of men and arms into South Vietnam.

There would be no more monotonous, month-long patrols scanning the skies with radar. Instead, these ships, built in World War II, would track and investigate thousands of the junks that motor and sail along the 1,200-mile coast of South Vietnam. This type of operation has not been carried out by the U.S. Navy since the Civil War, and before that since the days of Stephen Decatur during the War with Tripoli.

To the MARKET TIME forces, friend and foe are indistinguishable unless they are wearing an enemy uniform or are shooting. It is also very difficult to isolate contraband material, because items such as food and food preservatives are high on the Viet Cong priority list. How much rice or how much salt is too much for a single junk to be carrying? Inspection of a junk's papers is difficult, since forgery is easily accomplished. MARKET TIME forces must also be alert for draft dodgers and deserters, as the Viet Cong will employ them if they are not gainfully employed by the South Vietnamese government. The great majority of the junks that sail each day contain innocent tradesmen and fishermen, but those few that do not cause every junk to be stopped, boarded, and searched. This does not mean stopped once a week or once a month, but nearly every day, and in daylight or darkness.

For the DERs, this has made necessary a new shipboard organization, with many men qualifying in boarding crews and with more than the first division being trained in launching the whaleboat. The deck officers quickly become alert to fish traps, nets, unlighted junks, and the shallow, poorly charted coastal waters. The problem is compounded by monsoon winds and seas, and a tenacious and versatile enemy.

The commanding officer of a DER reporting for duty in one of these coastal areas will find himself faced with one of the most unusual situations he may ever encounter in his naval career. Instead of being handed a cumbersome, overly detailed operation order, which leaves little to the imagination and ingenuity of the commanding officer, he is given broad guide lines, consisting primarily of the rules of engagement, and a directive "to board and reboard all the junks he detects in his assigned area." In most cases his search encompasses thousands of square miles of water and hundreds of junks.

To accomplish his mission the commanding officer will be required to exercise every facet of his imagination, and to use every tool available; all his men must be positively motivated and mentally alert. If the tools are not on board, he must fabricate them if he is to accomplish his mission. While no two commanding officers approach the problem in the same way, the basic goal and requirement—to prevent infiltration and to board junks—must be the end result of every effort made. In one DER, for example, you will see in use a metal locator similar to that employed by a beachcomber in Malibu. Another ship uses a towing system for her whaleboat. In still another DER, an additional speedboat is used to increase boardings per day and save precious patrol time. Other tools of the trade include chemical testers, 24-inch searchlights, and new, electrically primed, 3-inch star shells.

The DER's commanding officer has a highly effective platform from which to carry out his mission. The original designers and the men who reconfigured these ships in the mid-1950s for their radar picket roles might well have had MARKET TIME–type operations in mind. With her economical diesel plant, the DER is not tied to an oiler's apron strings, and the ship has the range required to accomplish her search mission. The ship is well equipped and has electronics and communications matched by few other destroyer-type ships.

Although the DER has a relatively shallow navigational draft, she retains an effective ASW capability and can hurl 3-inch shells five miles. The 170 personnel on board are about optimum for consistent reliable operations. The ship is largely air conditioned, a great morale booster on the hot days and nights in the South China Sea or the Gulf of Siam. Few ships that are smaller than the DER can weather the monsoon storms and remain an aggressive unit night and day, hence the DER can remain on station when many smaller MARKET TIME units must seek a lee.

The DER has acted as mother ship for 83-foot Coast Guard patrol boats (WPB) and the 50-foot Navy Swift boats (PCF). Often two PCF crews and one PCF will be deployed with the DER, with the larger ship providing the lodging and logistics support to allow the PCF to remain away from her home base for extended periods. The DER also provides moral as well as gunfire support for the smaller patrol boats as they search areas too shallow for the DER. The fuel and lubricating oils required by these small craft are compatible with the DER and further improve the efficiency of the operation.

On occasion, the DER will enter port near the local coastal command center to be brought up to date on the detailed intelligence picture. In an operation like MARKET TIME, where weather, tactical considerations, enemy movements, and even the friendly forces available are so fluid and fluctuating, "old" information may mean a matter of hours or days. This center also provides a communications link with the Commander, Coastal Surveillance Force, in Saigon. Normally, the U.S. units in MARKET TIME are provided with Vietnamese liaison officers who provide local intelligence and serve as members of the junk boarding teams. These liaison officers on many occasions are able to obtain valuable intelligence data since they can speak fluently with the fishermen.

Operation MARKET TIME is what each DER makes it. The mission is clearly defined, the enemy is at hand, and the DER commanding officer is basically independent in accomplishing his mission, all of which offer an interesting challenge for all hands.

Lieutenant Commander W. J. Moredock, USN is currently the Commanding Officer of USS *Lowe* (DER-325).

"Cutters and Sampans"

4

Senior Chief Dennis L. Noble, USCG (Ret.)

U.S. Naval Institute *Proceedings*
(June 1984): 47–53

ON 10 MAY 1966, *the USCGC* Point Grey *(WPB-82324) was patrolling the east side of Ca Mau Peninsula when her crew spotted bonfires on the beach. While investigating the fires, the patrol boat picked up a steel-hulled target on her radar about six miles to seaward attempting to close the beach. The contact was tentatively identified as a 100-foot Chinese Nationalist vessel, traveling on a course of 260° at ten knots.*[1]

The Point Grey *began to shadow the trawler. At 0240, the trawler was within one mile of the beach opposite the fires, with three to four persons observed on deck. By 0500, the contact was within one-half mile of the beach, and the* Point Grey's *commanding officer notified his operational commander on the destroyer escort USS* Brister *(DER-327) that he would board the trawler at daylight.*

At 0700, the Point Grey *closed the trawler. The craft was found aground and deserted. As the men of the* Point Grey *attempted to board the trawler, they came under fire from the beach. The cutter moved out of small arms range and began to lob 81-mm. mortar rounds at the gun positions on the beach.*

For the next six hours, the Point Grey *kept the trawler under surveillance. At 1330, without air or naval gunfire support, the* Point Grey *again closed the trawler. At about 200 yards from the beach and within 100 yards of the trawler, the cutter came under "extremely" accurate small arms and automatic weapons fire.[2] Within 20 to 30 seconds, three of the four men on the bow of the* Point Grey *were hit: a coastguardsman, a U.S. Army major "along for the ride," and the South Vietnamese Navy liaison officer. Commissaryman Second Class Kepler was the first coastguardsman wounded in the Vietnam War.*

The cutter took about 25 hits, but no one was seriously hurt. Air strikes were called in to suppress the fire. The Point Grey's *crew then boarded the vessel.*

The haul from the trawler proved impressive. Contraband, including an estimated 50–60 tons of arms, ammunition, and supplies, was confiscated.

At 0100 on 14 March 1967, a patrol aircraft spotted a trawler 40 miles offshore and closing the beach. The Brister *began to track the contact by radar and assigned a fast patrol boat, PCF-78, to intercept.*

At 0530, PCF-78 reported that she was under heavy small arms and possible recoilless rifle fire, with many hits and one minor casualty. The USCGC Point Ellis *(WPB-82330) proceeded at high speed to assist.[3] She arrived at 0625 to find that the trawler had been beached.*

The Point Ellis *joined with the* Brister *in shelling the beach. While engaged in the gunfire mission, the commanding officer of the* Point Ellis, *Lieutenant (junior grade) Helton, maneuvered his cutter in a zigzag attack on the trawler. Suddenly, an explosion thundered across the water, and the trawler disappeared in a cloud of smoke. When the smoke cleared, only debris remained.*

Later, salvage operations recovered approximately 1,200 rifles, several machine guns, and miscellaneous ammunition. The Coast Guard War Diary *notes that "amazingly enough," no hits were taken by the* Point Ellis, *probably "attributable to the excellent manner" in which Helton handled his command.*

On 29 April 1965, newspaper readers were surprised to learn that units of the U.S. Coast Guard had been ordered to Vietnam. The U.S. Navy, the newspapers announced, had requested Coast Guard assistance in the form of 82-foot patrol boats. The deployment of these boats marks the beginning of the Coast Guard's role in the Vietnam War.

The Viet Cong were commonly perceived as elusive, silent figures, slipping through the night, living off the land, and, at battle time, mysteriously appearing with weapons cached in a hut or some other hiding place. True, the Viet Cong could live off the land, but they did need a supply line to obtain weapons, ammunition, and other material. The most direct route was the sea.[4]

In 1964, as insurgency increased, the North Vietnamese leaders in Hanoi made an important decision concerning the supply of forces in the south. Until this time, the insurgents had used French, British, and U.S. weapons. Under the new strategy, all arms would be standard, using the same caliber of ammunition, and more modem artillery would be employed. The most important weapon was the AK-47 Soviet assault rifle. Other new weapons included 7.62-mm. machine guns, rocket launchers (RPG-2s), 82-mm. Soviet and Chinese mortars, and 47- and 75-mm. recoilless rifles. This required an increase in infiltration.[5] The South Vietnamese Navy was pushed to the limit in trying to patrol 1,200 miles of coastline.

At 1030 on 16 February 1965, Lieutenant James S. Bowers, U.S. Army, flying a helicopter from Qui Nhon, sighted a camouflaged vessel in Vung Ro Bay on the central coast. Bowers radioed Second Coastal Zone Senior Adviser Lieutenant Commander Harvey P. Rogers, U.S. Navy, in Nha Trang.

The vessel, found carrying a large supply of arms and equipment, was engaged and sunk by the Navy. At last, U.S. advisers had proof of infiltration. More important, buried materiel was found nearby, proving that shipments had been increased.[6] The "Vung Ro Incident" led directly to Operation Market Time and the involvement of the U.S. Coast Guard's 82-foot patrol boats in Vietnam.[7]

On 3 March 1965, at the request of General William C. Westmoreland, a conference was held in South Vietnam to discuss seaborne infiltration. Those attending the conference decided that the "best tactic to interdict coastal traffic would be to assist and inspire the Vietnamese Navy to increase the quality and quantity of its searches."[8]

Infiltration of weapons and equipment by sea was accomplished in two ways: by coastwise junk traffic mingling with the more than 50,000 registered civilian craft plying Vietnam's coastal waters; and by vessels of trawler size (usually steel-hulled), which sailed innocently in international waters and, at a given location, would make a perpendicular approach to the coast. The trawlers probably originated in North Vietnam and the People's Republic of China.

To stop trawler infiltration, the conference members proposed that a conventional sea patrol be established by U.S. Navy ships and aircraft. They planned to establish a defensive area extending 40 miles to sea then have South Vietnam authorize U.S. naval forces to stop, board, and search vessels in its waters and the contiguous zone.

The Joint Chiefs of Staff approved the plan on 16 March. On 11 May, the South Vietnamese Government granted permission for Market Time units "to stop, search, and seize vessels not clearly engaged in innocent passage inside the three-mile limit of the Republic of Vietnam's territorial waters."[9] Operation Market Time was now under way.

Market Time operations were divided into nine patrol areas, stretching from the 17th parallel to the Brevie Line in the Gulf of Thailand.[10] Normally, a destroyer escort (radar) or an oceangoing minesweeper was responsible for each patrol area. Five coastal surveillance centers, Da Nang, Qui Nhon, Nha Trang, Vung Tau, and An Thoi, were responsible for coordinating patrol units.[11]

On 16 April 1965, with Market Time planning in full swing, Secretary of the Navy Paul Nitze requested Secretary of the Treasury Henry H. Fowler to inform him on the availability of U.S. Coast Guard units to deploy to Vietnam. Three days later, the Commandant of the Coast Guard informed the Navy Department that 82-foot and 40-foot patrol boats were available. After a meeting between Navy and Coast Guard officials, the Coast Guard agreed to deploy 17 82-foot patrol boats. The official joint memorandum to the President was sent on 29 April, advising him of the deployment. The next day, U.S. Coast Guard Squadron One was formed.[12]

The patrol boat was ideal for Market Time. She had unique design features that allowed for a small peacetime complement of eight men. The machinery was designed to facilitate underway operations without a continuous engine room watch. Engine speed was controlled by throttles on the bridge. Main engine and generator alarms were also mounted in the wheelhouse. The bridge was designed so that all navigation equipment, radio, radar, and engine controls were centered on a console about the wheel. If necessary, one man could steer, control the speed, guard the radar, observe the Fathometer, and operate the radio. This ability was especially useful when most of the crew was on deck during operations.

The patrol boat was twin-screwed, propelled by two turbo-charged, 600-shaft horsepower VT-12M Cummings diesel engines, one on each shaft. The hull was constructed of black steel and had six water-tight compartments. The superstructure was built of aluminum. The patrol boat displaced 65 tons and, most important, drew only six feet of water.

Finally, she could berth and mess a crew for a short period of time. This craft was the only shallow-water patrol boat that had this ability, thus, she could remain on patrol for longer periods of time.

The patrol boats were modified for their combat role. A 50-caliber machine gun was mounted on top of an 81-mm. mortar. This piggyback armament was then placed on the boat's bow. Four additional 50-caliber machine guns were installed on the main deck, aft the wheelhouse. Ready service boxes were installed on deck to store the additional ammunition. Other changes ranged from better reefers to more bunks.

On 6 May 1965, the 17 patrol boats were loaded as deck cargo on merchant ships in New York, Norfolk, New Orleans, Galveston, San Pedro, San Francisco, and Seattle. Five days later, coastguardsmen began to report to the West Coast for training.

Initially, 47 officers and 198 enlisted men formed Coast Guard Squadron One. Their four weeks of training consisted of courses in gunnery, communications, escape and evasion, and other military training. After training, the men joined their patrol boats in Subic Bay.

At Subic Bay, the patrol boats received last-minute modifications, crews were assigned, and the squadron was organized. It was divided into two divisions. Division Eleven consisted of eight boats; Division Twelve received the remainder. Division Twelve sailed for Da Nang on 15 July, arriving five days later. Division Eleven sailed on 20 July and arrived at An Thoi on 31 July.[13]

The cutters, as were all Market Time surface units, were expected to "conduct surveillance, gunfire support, visit and search, and other operations as directed along the coast of the Republic of Vietnam in order to assist the Republic of Vietnam in detection and prevention of Communist infiltration from the seas."[14] Because of the many junks, sampans, and other craft in the area, a priority system of boarding had to be established. A ranking of boardings was developed with the following scheme: vessels transiting the area, junks fishing or operating in restricted areas, fishing boats anchored and not working nets, and last, fishing boats working nets.[15]

When ready for patrol, a cutter would report to the minesweeper or destroyer escort maintaining outer barrier patrol. The outer patrol would provide radar and navigational assistance to the cutter. In a like manner, the cutter would provide the same information to South Vietnamese Navy junk units working close to the beach. In the Gulf of Thailand, six of the nine patrol boats were constantly on patrol, each in one of six designated subareas. The boats were under way for four days, and then they returned to the support ship for two days. Each boat rotated through all the subareas.[16]

Life on board the small patrol boats was rough. The crews usually worked from 12 to 16 hours a day when under way. In the Gulf of Thailand area, for instance, the boats had a three-section watch: three men—the officer-of-the-deck, helmsman, and radioman—stood a four-hour watch; a second section served as boarding party; and a third would be off duty. The captain and cook stood no watches. An officer was on hand for all boardings. The men had to be on guard constantly. Any common fishing craft could suddenly open fire with automatic weapons. Eventually, most crew members learned the maxim: "Don't relax. It could mean your life!"[17]

On her first patrol near the 17th parallel, the USCGC *Point Orient* (WPB-82319) came under mortar and machine gun fire. In an incredible oversight, the cutter was still painted her peacetime color of white. As one officer said, "White cutters are a beautiful sight on a moonlit or flarelit night, that is, unless you are on the cutter."[18] The next day, the boats began to be repainted.

When not under way, the patrol boats moored alongside a support ship. While lying to, the coastguardsmen painted, repaired, and took on supplies for the next patrol. The sailors had little time to relax. Moreover, there were no recreational facilities in the boats. Therefore, the Commander Squadron One had two spare boat crews so that each man could have five days of rest and recreation every three months.[19]

One Market Time operational policy did not set well with many coastguardsmen. The Navy's Swift boats were not suited for offshore work in adverse weather. The Coast Guard patrol boats, however, could weather many storms. In September 1967, the Market Time Commander decided that the Coast Guard boats should shift with the seasons. In other words, Coast Guard patrol boats followed the monsoons, while the Navy Swifts followed the sunshine.[20]

In the first month of patrols, the cutter crews boarded more than 1,100 junks and sampans, inspected more than 4,000 Vietnamese craft, and worked more than 4,800 man-hours. To counter the cutters' efforts, the Viet Cong told local fishermen that the U.S. boats were driving them from the best fishing grounds so that U.S. fishing boats could fish there. Indeed, this must have appeared true, for the best fishing grounds were frequently in restricted waters, and the cutters had to displace the fishermen. To counter this move by the Viet Cong, the U.S. Coast Guard,

Navy, and South Vietnamese developed a program to help the fishermen, which included medical care.

By October 1965, it became apparent that Market Time forces were spread too thin, especially along Vietnam's southeast coast. On 29 October 1965, Secretary of the Navy Nitze requested an additional nine cutters be deployed to Vietnam. This group, Division Thirteen, took station at Vung Tau in early 1966.[21]

The year was a busy and dangerous one for the men of the small cutters. The USCGC *Point White* (WPB-82308), only in-country for a month, was patrolling in the Soi Rap River area. The cutter's customary operations method was to steam into her area "to show the flag," steam out, and then try to covertly reenter the area. On this occasion, the ruse worked, for the cutter spotted a junk crossing the river and attempted to halt the craft. The junk opened fire with automatic weapons and small arms. The *Point White* returned fire and rammed the junk, throwing the hostile vessel's crew into the water. One of the junk's passengers was a key Viet Cong leader of the Rung Sat Zone.

But junks and sampans were not the only craft firing on the cutters. On the night of 11 August 1966, the USCGC *Point Welcome* (WPB-82329) steamed near the demilitarized zone.[22] Suddenly, the cutter was illuminated and under attack by friendly aircraft. Several hits ripped into the wheelhouse. A gasoline fire blazed on deck. The crew tried to fight the fire and repel the attack simultaneously. Finally, there was nothing to do but run the cutter aground and abandon her.

Later, other Coast Guard units arrived on scene to assist the *Point Welcome*. The rescue units found the commanding officer of the cutter and one crew member dead. The executive officer, two other crewmen, the South Vietnamese liaison officer, and a *Life* magazine reporter were wounded. The *Point Welcome* was refloated and towed to port for repairs.

At the beginning of Operation Market Time, the Chief of the Naval Advisory Group, Rear Admiral Norvell G. Ward, foresaw the necessity of returning the responsibility of naval operations to the South Vietnamese

Navy. His command and control decisions were therefore predicated upon training South Vietnamese to eventually relieve U.S. forces.[23]

Vice Admiral Elmo R. Zumwalt, Jr., upon assuming command as Commander Naval Forces, Vietnam, on 30 September 1968, concentrated on developing an accelerated plan to transfer U.S. Navy equipment to the South Vietnamese. In 1969, two South Vietnamese Navy lieutenants reported on board patrol boats, initiating the first phase of the turnover program. One month later, 17 South Vietnamese Navy ensigns and two lieutenants reported to Squadron One. On 16 May 1969, the USCGC *Point Garnet* (WPB-82310) and *Point League* (WPB-82304) were transferred to the South Vietnamese Navy at Saigon and renamed the *Le Phuoc Duc* and *Le Van Nga,* respectively. On 15 August 1970, the last of the 26 cutters were transferred to the South Vietnamese Navy. This ended the role of the 82-foot U.S. Coast Guard cutters in Vietnam.[24]

The statistics of Coast Guard Squadron One are impressive. The Coast Guard boarded 236,396 junks and sampans, inspected 283,527 vessels, participated in 4,461 naval gunfire missions, cruised 4,215,116 miles, damaged or destroyed 1,811 vessels, and wounded or killed 1,055 of the enemy. The Coast Guard casualties were seven killed and 53 wounded.[25] Most important, the cutters helped shift the enemy's supply route. General Westmoreland noted that before 1965 an estimated 70% of the enemy's supplies arrived by sea; "by the end of 1966, our best guess was not more than 10 percent" arrived by sea.[26]

The Coast Guard's involvement in Vietnam was not restricted to the 82-foot patrol boats. At sea, 56 different combat cutters, including high-endurance cutters, were assigned to Vietnamese waters. Noncombat cutters also participated in the war. For example, four buoy tenders and one cargo vessel were assigned to Vietnam. The buoy tenders assisted in aids-to-navigation duties, such as setting buoys and other markers for the safe navigation of ships. Shore units included port security, which supervised the loading and unloading of dangerous cargoes. Also, shipping advisers and Merchant Marine details helped merchant shipping.

But Operation Market Time proved the military ability of the U.S. Coast Guard. This small service was able to go from its peacetime role of search and rescue to war halfway around the world in less than 75 days. The Coast Guard performed and worked effectively with other services and played a major role in actions requiring small craft. In short, the U.S. Coast Guard proved the truth of *Semper Paratus.*

Notes

1. Information on the *Point Grey*'s engagement from Commander, *Coast Guard Squadron One Diary,* 1–15 May 1966, Navy Operational Archives, Naval Historical Center, Washington, D.C.
2. James A. Hodgman, "Market Time in the Gulf of Thailand," *Proceedings,* May 1968, pp. 39–40; Commander, *Coast Guard Squadron One Diary.*
3. Information on the *Point Ellis*'s engagement from Commander, *Coast Guard Squadron One Diary,* 14 March 1967.
4. R. L. Schreadley, "The Naval War in Vietnam, 1950–1970," *Proceedings,* May 1971, p. 182; W. C. Westmoreland, *Report on Operations in South Vietnam, January 1964–June 1968* (Washington, D.C.: U.S. Government Printing Office, 1969), p. 128.
5. Westmoreland, pp. 87–88.
6. Schreadley, p. 187.
7. Schreadley, pp. 186–187; Eugene N. Tullich, *The United States Coast Guard in Southeast Asia During the Vietnam Conflict* (Washington, D.C.: Public Affairs Division, U.S. Coast Guard, 1975), p. 1.
8. Schreadley, p. 188.
9. Ibid.
10. The Brevie Line is the geographic division in the Gulf of Thailand between Vietnam and Cambodia. Islands and territorial waters to the north of that line are Cambodian and to the south, Vietnamese. Schreadley, p. 190.
11. Ibid.
12. Hodgman, pp. 39–40.
13. Hodgman, pp. 40–45; Tullich, pp. 3–5.
14. Schreadley, p. 190.
15. Tullich, p. 5.
16. Ibid.
17. Hodgman, p. 49.
18. Tullich, p. 6.
19. Hodgman, pp. 53–54.
20. Tullich, p. 12.
21. Ibid., pp. 6–8.

22. Information on the *Point Welcome* from Tullich, p. 10.
23. Schreadley, p. 191.
24. Schreadley, pp. 197–198; Tullich, pp. 14–15.
25. Tullich, p. 55.
26. Westmoreland, p. 128.

AUTHOR'S NOTE: *I wish to thank Professor Robert E. May, Department of History, and Kevin Reid, Department of History, Purdue University, for their helpful comments.*

Senior Chief Noble entered the U.S. Coast Guard in 1957 and retired in 1978 as a Senior Chief Marine Science Technician. He received bachelor's and master's degrees from the Catholic University of America, Washington, D.C. Since retirement, he has been the Director of the Delphi Public Library, Indiana, and he is studying for his doctorate degree in U.S. history at Purdue University. Senior Chief Noble is the coauthor of two books and author or coauthor of more than 20 articles.

"Skimmer Ops"

5

Lieutenant J. F. Ebersole, USCG

U.S. Naval Institute *Proceedings*
(July 1974): 40–46

FROM THE TIME OF THEIR ARRIVAL in Vietnamese waters in July 1965, the primary mission of the 82-foot patrol boats (WPBs) of Coast Guard Squadron One was to prevent enemy infiltration by sea. Serving as part of the U.S. Navy's "Market Time"–patrol force (CTF 115), the Squadron's 26 WPBs were responsible for the security of a major portion of South Vietnam's 750-mile coastline and eventually became participants in the river war as well.

To meet their king-sized offshore responsibility, the units of CTF 115 used a vigorous board and search campaign for the thousands of sampans and junks which could be found plying the coastal waters of Vietnam at any given time. From Da Nang to An Thoi, a variety of watercraft (from reed basket boats to steel-hulled trawlers) were found along the coast engaged in the nation's commerce, carrying fish or produce to and from market, and transporting the fisherman in search of his daily catch. But, some of these same craft were also known to be transporting men and munitions to North Vietnamese and Viet Cong units along the coast.

The discovery in February 1965 of a 130-foot junk off-loading enemy supplies in Vung Ro Bay brought about the decision to order the Coast Guard patrol vessels to Vietnam. In this particular case, the camouflaged junk had infiltrated with enough arms and supplies to outfit an entire enemy battalion. There were reasons to believe that similar landings were being made at other points along the coast.

During their first year of operation in the South China Sea and Gulf of Thailand, the Coast Guard units inspected or boarded over 65,000 junks and sampans. In so doing, they discovered some 250 tons of munitions as well as food and medical supplies intended for the VC, and detained hundreds of Viet Cong suspects. In compiling this impressive record, the WPB crews quickly learned that their part in the war was to have little glamour.

The routine boarding was a hot, dirty, and monotonous job. It was normal procedure for the boarding party, one or two Coast Guardsmen and a Vietnamese Navy liaison officer, or petty officer, to make a complete search of the vessel, its cargo (including fish) and, in some cases, its crew to determine the presence of any contraband. Often, the search would include a check for a double bottom (several were found in the Mekong Delta region) and even an inspection of the keel by rigging a line under the junk's hull and pulling it from stem to stern to detect any unusual underwater appendages or trailing lines. The identification papers of all persons on board and the vessel's papers, if commercially operated, were examined closely by the VNN liaison for authenticity. Those without papers, or with expired or otherwise suspect papers, were detained for questioning by Vietnamese Navy officials at one of their bases along the coast.

Depending upon the size craft, cargo, number of persons on board, and the availability of a metal detector to the boarding party (particularly valuable in searching large cargoes of rice), a thorough boarding would take from 10 to 30 minutes or more to complete. This procedure was repeated many times during a day, a month, a year, and often under less than ideal conditions. Choppy seas, pungent bilges (nuoc mom, the odoriferous fish sauce that was a part of every Vietnamese's diet, was everywhere) and difficulties in translating instructions could, and often did, complicate and lengthen the boardings.

An "inspection" differed from a boarding in that it usually entailed only a visual examination from alongside and a check of the personal identification papers. A crewman did not actually board unless something suspicious was noted. This procedure was reserved for use with the smaller, open sampans and basket boats where boarding could pose a danger of capsizing (which did occur from time to time, even in the larger sampans.)

At first, both the boardings and inspections performed by the Coast Guard were done only from the deck of the 82-footer. This provided a high degree of security, as a modified general quarters condition was maintained during such operations, and it provided a relatively stable platform from which to work. However, several disadvantages also became apparent:

- delays in bringing the Vietnamese alongside (notoriously bad ship handlers, for the most part) reduced the number of boardings possible to a small percentage of the total vessels in many areas;
- delays in clearing the side again also occurred frequently, particularly if two or more junks were tied abreast;
- reduced mobility for the WPB owing to junks alongside for examination precluded a quick response to evading craft; and
- inability to move with the concentrations of fishing vessels because of reduced mobility while boarding.

Recognizing the need for a more rapid and efficient way in which to carry out these boardings, the Coast Guard cutter's small boat was pressed into service—the diminutive 13-foot, fiberglass Boston Whaler that is familiar to many Americans as a standard recreational vehicle for fishing and water sports. Fitted with a steering wheel and a 40-h.p. outboard engine, this boat was identical to those manufactured for the pleasure craft market except for a coat of grey paint.

Nicknamed "skimmers" in recognition of their ability to skim along the top of the water at high speeds (up to 40 m.p.h.), this and similar type boats proved to be invaluable in a variety of missions. It provided the WPB with new flexibility in boarding procedures. For the first time the small boat, or skimmer, was used to "round up" the sampans and junks in an area and direct them to the parent vessel from which the boarding was accomplished. In areas of restricted maneuverability, such as narrow river mouths or where rocks and shoals were known to be present, this tactic allowed the cutter to anchor while the skimmer rounded up the sampans and junks.

Another procedure commonly used was to board or inspect directly from the small boat. Because of its superior speed and maneuverability, the outboard was able to move from junk to junk much more quickly than the WPB. Additionally, in those cases where a sampan or junk attempted to evade inspection by running or entering shallow water, the speedy Whaler was invaluable for its ability to pursue and apprehend.

When boarding, the skimmer would go alongside the vessel to be examined, putting the liaison/boarding officer aboard, and then laying off while the examination was conducted. By standing clear, the small boat could more effectively provide cover (as did the patrol boat). This also minimized possible damage from the boats beating together and kept the skimmer out of grenade range.

With either of these methods of boarding, or a combination whereby the skimmer and the WPB were boarding simultaneously, it was possible to conduct a thorough examination of a hundred or more craft per day (a large increase over the WPB-only procedure). However, when the 82-footer and skimmer were both boarding, it was important that the two work in close proximity so that the skimmer would not be endangered by the WPB's reduced reaction time.

When using the skimmer for boarding or other operations, sea conditions were a prime concern. The 13-foot Boston Whaler proved itself to be an extremely rugged and seaworthy boat when properly handled.

It was successfully launched and recovered in seas of six to eight feet. However, this was certainly the exception. A chop of two to three feet was considered a maximum for most operations.

The comparatively light weight and small size of the 13-foot skimmer made it easy to handle and secure aboard the 82-footer even in fairly heavy seas. But, these same features imposed limitations in its use. Personnel and equipment had to be kept to a bare minimum to prevent swamping and to prevent loss of crucial speed and maneuverability.

In selecting the skimmer's crew, an experienced leading petty officer and an engineer were assigned to accompany the VNN liaison who made most of the boardings. Each of these men was equipped with an automatic weapon. The liaison officer and the Coast Guard boarding petty officer usually carried only a sidearm to keep both hands free for transferring from boat to boat. The coxswain, who stood-off during the boarding, would cover with an M-16.

Each member was also equipped with a helmet and a floatable flak jacket. The latter provided dual protection from shrapnel and a dunking; however, because of bulkiness and the heat, they were never popular items. Many crews eventually shunned the flak jacket entirely for routine boardings and carried a Mae West type inflatable life vest when in the skimmer.

Other equipment for the small boat included a flak jacket to wrap each gas tank, a portable radio, anchor and line, pop flares, a first aid kit (primarily for treating minor injuries among the Vietnamese boarded), a few basic tools for the engineer, psychological warfare operations (Psyops) material for distribution to those examined, and the "Junk Log." The PsyOps material provided normally included soap, government propaganda leaflets, South Vietnamese flags, and occasionally candy for the children. The WPB's commissary also provided apples, oranges, and other fresh fruit which, on the whole, proved to be the most popular.

The "Junk Log" was a ledger in which each vessel boarded or inspected was listed. Also included were any unusual circumstances that might bear reporting or continued observation.

Through its service in offshore boarding and PsyOps operations, the skimmer gained a reputation for versatility and endurance which was put to the test on the inland and coastal waterways.

As Commander R. L. Schreadley, U.S. Navy, pointed out in "Sea Lords" *(Proceedings,* August 1970), "By almost all measurable criteria the task forces [Market Time, Game Warden, and Mobile Riverine] had achieved a high degree of effectiveness [by the fall of 1968]. There had been no known attempts to infiltrate large shipments of men or arms into South Vietnam by sea since the Tet offensive earlier in the year. Possibly, small intra-coastal transhipments may still have occurred, but if they did, it was at a high cost to the enemy because of the intensive and well co-ordinated Market Time air and sea patrols. These patrols had forced the enemy to reorient his entire logistics system and to organize and construct networks of infiltration routes in the Demilitarized Zone, in Laos, and in Cambodia." In the words of one Market Time Swift boat (PCF) skipper, "If we hadn't done *our* job so well, they wouldn't have had to build the Ho Chi Minh Trail."

As the emphasis on interdiction of the enemy's supply lines shifted inland in late 1968, many of the Market Time units found themselves a part of the inland Sea Lord operation. This was particularly true of the cutters assigned to Coast Guard Division 13 at Cat Lo.

Located just north of the rice-rich Mekong Delta, with its intricate network of rivers and canals, the WPBs and PCFs at Cat Lo became increasingly active in operations along the intra-coastal waterways. These Market Time units were frequently assigned to Sea Lord missions which took them up to 20 miles inland from their normal coastal patrol areas.

Working in such rivers as the Ham Luong, Co Chien, the mighty Bassac and the treacherous Ganh Hao, the WPBs of Division 13 and their PCF counterparts found themselves at work in some of the strongest Viet Cong sanctuaries in the Delta. These enemy strongholds included the Rung Sat, Thanh Phu, and Long Toan Special (or "Secret") Zones and the inhospitable Dung Island Complex.

Operations included intelligence gathering, troop insertions, harassment and interdiction, and an inland version of the familiar board and search. To be effective in these missions, surprise and quick response were essential. These were often difficult to achieve, especially when working in the smaller canals. While often 30 to 40 feet in depth, many of the canals running through the Special Zones were less than 100 feet wide. An 82-footer transiting such waters, with her prominent superstructure and mast visible above the bordering tree lines, might well have appeared to be some waterborne behemoth to enemy eyes, but hard to detect she was not; nor was the smaller, but noisier, Swift boat with its distinctive engine exhaust.

As for quick response, these seagoing patrol craft were again hampered in the more restricted canals. The PCF, being some 30 feet shorter and 10 to 15 knots faster, was the more agile of the two, but even the Swift boat had difficulty in pursuing the enemy's motorized sampans and junks on the narrow, winding tributaries. This point was driven home to one PCF skipper in the heart of the Thanh Phu Secret Zone. As he attempted to apprehend an evading sampan at high speed, he failed to negotiate a sharp turn in the monsoon-swollen canal, cleared the bank, and found himself hard aground in an adjacent rice paddy.

Reports of WPBs having to back out of unfriendly canals to find room enough to turn around; losing whip radio antennas to overhanging trees; and engaging the enemy through the use of spotters looking over the tree lines from exposed perches atop the cutter's mast were not uncommon. However, they were received with mixed feelings by the cognizant operational commanders. While admiring the courage and tenacity of the units involved, the extreme dangers were also recognized. There had to be a better way.

Here was another area in which the skimmer could be of assistance. The Coast Guard patrol boats had continued to use their small boats for board and search work after moving into the river mouths. This, coupled with the limited experiences gained in using the small boats as waterborne guard posts during their offshore patrols (keeping an eye on suspected enemy landing points along the coast), enabled the Coast Guard units to make an easy transition to the requirements for Sea Lord skimmer operations.

With an outboard or two in company, it was much easier for the WPBs and PCFs to probe the many small canals which laced the VC controlled Secret Zones and had proven so troublesome in the past. The speedy skimmers enjoyed a much higher success rate than had their parent units (by way of clarification, the PCFs did not carry a small boat) in surprising and engaging the enemy. Unfriendly small craft and personnel ashore were often caught unexpectedly as a skimmer appeared suddenly around a canal bend in advance of the covering patrol craft. The Whalers were also effective in detecting camouflaged VC small craft and supplies along the canal banks, and in probing connecting waterways, too narrow for the covering unit to turn around in.

Certain safeguards were employed in all small boat operations. The skimmer was always accompanied by another unit when probing a canal (a "two unit minimum" doctrine also applied to PCF and WPB canal operations). A single skimmer was not allowed to operate in canals where the parent WPB could not cover, and, if necessary, enter and physically remove the boat. When using two or more small boats, they were staggered and assigned to opposite banks to minimize the effects of possible enemy ambushes.

Some of the WPBs' greatest results in detecting and disrupting the enemy's in-shore movements occurred in conjunction with nighttime small boat operations. Typical of these was the covert surveillance operation. A skimmer would be launched by an 82-footer well clear of a suspected VC position and then be towed into the vicinity so that only the single unit was heard. Once the small boat was cast free the WPB would proceed out of the immediate area leaving the impression of a routine transit. The skimmer was then either anchored or paddled into shore (using a compass or the starlight scope to navigate). Once in position, a listening and visual surveillance was maintained, often for the entire night. If enemy activity was detected this was reported to the supporting unit(s) by radio, using a set equipped with a pilot's helmet-type head set to prevent detection.

The experiences of one such skimmer guard post illustrates the value and the hazards of this type operation. Late in 1969, the cutter *Point Grace* launched a surveillance skimmer in the Co Chien River which detected a great deal of nocturnal activity in an adjoining section of the Long Toan Secret Zone. Anchored in the mouth of a canal which flowed from the Zone into the river, the small boat crew detected a number of male Vietnamese voices and caught occasional glimpses of movement along a nearby embankment through the starlight scope. Their surveillance was cut short, however, by the sudden appearance of a small motorized sampan exiting the canal. With neither showing lights or expecting the other, a collision nearly resulted. In the ensuing excitement the sampan was halted and found to be carrying a very surprised, unarmed man and woman. As they had no identification they were escorted to the *Point Grace* for detainment and eventual delivery to a VNN Coastal Group. They were later identified as Communist sympathizers.

In apprehending the sampan, the skimmer had revealed its presence to those heard earlier on shore. Thus, when the small boat attempted to resume its watch, it was welcomed with a barrage of automatic weapons fire. In the fire fight which followed, the skimmer was able to clear the area (with several holes but no casualties) under the *Point Grace's* protective umbrella of .50 caliber fire. Subsequent daylight mortar fire from the *Point Grace* and an air strike by the highly regarded "Black Ponies" (OV-10) of Vung Tau-based VAL-4 resulted in a number of secondary explosions and heavy black smoke. An enemy supply point had been detected and destroyed, thanks to a 13-foot "fishing" boat.

Skimmer operations similar to those conducted by the Coast Guard were also performed by the U.S. and Vietnamese Navy personnel assigned to the Coastal Groups in the Delta. While most Coastal Groups served primarily as bases for the Vietnamese Navy's junk force, the U.S. Navy advisory staffs at the bases on the Ham Luong, Co Chien, and Bassac rivers were also equipped with 22-foot Kenner Ski Barges. These were beamy, flat bottomed, twin outboard skimmers which also emerged from the U.S. recreational boat market. They boasted considerably more room and speed than the 13-foot Boston Whaler.

Inasmuch as the Coastal Groups normally had but one of these skimmers assigned, the offer of a WPB Whaler for a joint operation was welcomed by the senior U.S. Navy advisor. Also working under a two-unit doctrine, the addition of an experienced Coast Guard crew and skimmer permitted the Coastal Group to mount probes and surveillance operations in the more hostile regions of their areas of responsibility. It also permitted board and search activities to be conducted in the more shoal reaches of the rivers where WPBs, PCFs, and VNN junks alike were barred by their draft.

One result of these joint WPB-Coastal Group skimmer operations for the Coast Guard was the recognized value in having a larger, twin-engine boat for particularly hazardous missions. The greater size permitted the assigning of additional weapons while the extra engine provided both speed and a back-up in case of engine failure.

To capitalize on this experience, two 17-foot Boston Whalers, one with dual 40-h.p. outboards, the other with a single 85-h.p. engine, were placed into service as Coast Guard Division 13's "special ops" boats. Unlike the Kenner boat, these big brothers of the 13-foot Whaler were capable of being carried aboard and launched from an 82-footer without any modification to the WPBs boat cradle or boom.

The "special ops" boats were armed with a twin M-60 machine gun mounted forward and single M-60s mounted on the sides. The twin mount on one of these boats was replaced in the spring of 1970 with an aircraft type "mini-gun" that was "borrowed" from the Air Force. However, use of this sophisticated weapon proved to be a short-lived experiment as its rapid rate of fire advantage was offset by a temperamental nature and an inability to carry enough ammunition in the small boat to realize its full potential. Nonetheless, for several operations the Viet Cong must have been impressed by the fire (every fourth round a tracer) which originated from the head of this waterborne "baby dragon."

To man the 17-footers for offensive or hazardous missions, the boat was assigned a crew of five—a boat officer (usually the WPB's CO or XO), an engineer, a gunner's mate, and two others. This provided three gunners, a radio operator (the boat officer), and a coxswain.

The 17-foot Whaler offered other advantages in addition to those already mentioned. Its "cathedral" style hull provided a higher degree of seaworthiness than found in either of its previously mentioned contemporaries; this permitted its use in unprotected waters and in more severe sea conditions. Its size permitted an increase in passenger load which was invaluable during troop insertions and extractions.

Reminiscent of one of the Coast Guard's roles in World War II, the WPBs frequently found themselves acting as a type of amphibious assault vessel, landing and removing ground troops from enemy soil. Both U.S. and Vietnamese army troops were teamed with the 82-footers and their skimmers to carry out probes of enemy territory, particularly the more remote regions where overland travel was difficult or impossible and where insertion by air could preclude essential surprise.

Between 30 and 40 troops, most often Vietnamese with U.S. Army advisors, and their equipment was a typical force for a single cutter. These troops would be landed at a given site either by placing the WPB's bow into the bank (if in a canal or river) LST style, or by using the skimmers if in shallow water. Once ashore, the ground force could conduct a sweep of the area while the patrol boat provided gun fire support and the skimmers conducted a "blocking" action to prevent any enemy escape from the sweep zone via water. If the troops were caught in an ambush, the skimmer provided a way out. Many an outnumbered allied force found it necessary to take advantage of the skimmer's fast ride to the safety of a covering WPB. The outboard's low profile, speed, and maneuverability (even though reduced by a load of up to a dozen troops), made for an elusive target during such "extractions."

Whether rescuing trapped soldiers on unfriendly beaches or rounding up sampans for routine inspections, the small boat saw increasingly important and varied use until the time of U.S. withdrawal from Vietnam. Criticized by some as a craft dangerously vulnerable to both combat and the natural elements, the skimmers achieved their successes as a result of the thorough planning, sound judgment, courage, and skill of those who manned them.

The Coast Guard skimmer ended its role in Vietnam with the disestablishment of Coast Guard Division 13 in August of 1970. Turned over to the Vietnamese Navy along with the last of the original 26 WPBs, these versatile skimmers will be remembered for their contributions to the war afloat.

A former enlisted man, **Lieutenant Ebersole** is a 1967 graduate of Coast Guard OCS. On commissioning, he was assigned to the CGC *Chilula* he served as Communications and Operations Officer. From June 1968 to June 1969 he commanded the patrol boat CGC *Cape Morgan* at Charleston, S.C. This was followed by assignment to CG Division 13 at Cat Lo, Vietnam, where he served as commanding officer of the CGC *Point Grace* and as Division Operations Officer. His Vietnam tour was followed by a three-year assignment to Coast Guard Headquarters where he assumed duties as Chief, Training Branch, Office of Boating Safety. Since July 1973 he has been assigned as XO of CGC *Laurel*, Morehead City, N.C.

"Trawler!"

6

Commander Charles R. Stephan, USN

U.S. Naval Institute *Proceedings*
(September 1968): 60–81

AT 1925 ON 11 JULY 1967, the pilot of patrol aircraft No. 10, Patrol Squadron One, reported to Market Time Coastal Surveillance Center in Da Nang that he had contact with a small steel-hulled trawler headed on a course of 220 degrees, at a speed of 10 knots, and located 55 miles east of Chu Lai. That information in itself was enough to send CSC to "General Quarters." Any ship which closes the South Vietnam shoreline on a perpendicular course is suspect. The P2 had flown low enough to read the numerals "459" on the trawler's bow. The pilot had reported further that the unmarked trawler had a "large crate on deck" and was running dark. The sun had just set, so that "running dark" was not necessarily unusual. At CSC, the trawler was plotted on the Market Time tactical plot. Her track was projected to determine which ship in the barrier patrol should be vectored to intercept. The U.S. radar picket escort ship, *Wilhoite* (DER-397) was steaming on the southern barrier at a point where the trawler's projected track crossed the barrier line and, thus, was directed to "maintain present station until further ordered."

An hour later, the P2 returned to check on the trawler and found that she had turned on her running lights and had changed course to 120 degrees, a significantly suspicious action. With this move, the *Wilhoite* was ordered to close and make contact, but to observe covertly. The *Wilhoite* pursued, made radar contact, and, after a careful handoff from the aircraft, took over the duties of shadowing the trawler. For good measure, however, the relief aircraft, No. 7, continued to track during the night. After daylight next morning, the *Wilhoite* was ordered to close for an identification run and to take pictures. The aircraft did likewise. The *Wilhoite* reported a dark green trawler about 120 feet long with the bow number 459. Fishing gear and nets were distributed topside. There was no sign of a crate. No identification or indication of nationality was visible, and the three men on deck paid no attention to the ship as she made a circle around the freighter, then headed off over the horizon to resume radar tracking. The trawler carried no radar or any other visible sophisticated electronics equipment.

At Saigon, the Market Time Task Force Commander directed the *Wilhoite* to continue covert surveillance "all the way back to Haiphong, if necessary." It was anticipated that the trawler's captain would probably resume his infiltration attempt when he thought he had shaken off his pursuers. During the night he had taken an easterly course, to a location southeast of the Paracel Islands. He then turned north and steamed up to a point where, at 1300 on the 13th, he anchored for three hours, then got underway and started to retrace his track. The *Wilhoite* held station just out of visual range. So it was that on the night of 13 July, 2300 by Da Nang time, the trawler appeared to be headed back for the area where she had been detected initially.

This was not the first such incident. Four months before, on 14 March 1967, another trawler had attempted to infiltrate this same area. Again, the trawler had been detected initially by Market Time patrol aircraft. In the ensuing hours, surface units of the Market Time force had taken station near the trawler and had forced her ashore. She had beached at about 0600 local time. In those latitudes, it is still very dark at that hour in March. While Market Time ships fired illumination rounds and suppressive fire at the beach to keep the trawler from being unloaded, plans were being made to board her. Suddenly, at 0630, the ship exploded with such cataclysmic violence that tiny pieces were scattered for a thousand yards in all directions. There was hardly enough of the ship left to be recognizable. Not a single weapon on the trawler remained useable. There was little question, therefore, but that the July trawler was similarly rigged and could be expected to destroy herself *if not captured before the crew could abandon her.*

The staff of the Northern Surveillance Group, of which I had been designated the Commander, assembled late in the evening of the 13th when we were sure the trawler was returning to the Cape Batangan area and began planning for the operation that would almost surely take place the next night. The speed of the trawler at that time would have brought her ashore at about 2000 on the 14th, but this was ruled out as a possibility because the moon would still have been up, and though it was not yet full, it was too bright to risk being seen. It was reasoned that she would slow up during the late afternoon and try for the beach after moonset, a little after midnight. To disarm the destructive charge which the trawler probably carried, Naval Support Activity, Da Nang, was asked to provide an Explosive Ordnance Demolition specialist.

That same evening the new U.S. gunboat *Gallup* (PG-85) had arrived for duty with the Northern Surveillance Group. She was to depart for patrol off the Quang Ngai coast the next day. With the very high speed available from the *Gallup's* turbine power, I decided to spend most of the day in Da Nang watching the movements of the trawler, complete plans for the operation, then leave late in the afternoon in time to transit in the *Gallup* to rendezvous with the *Wilhoite,* transferring to that ship as On Scene Commander. The *Wilhoite,* after nearly three days of tracking the trawler, had proven that her CIG and operations team was superb, as were her communications. The *Gallup's* participation in the operation was most welcome for several reasons. Her 3-inch and 40-mm. guns would provide important firepower, her speed might be extremely useful in some unpredicted emergency, in addition to permitting a last-minute departure from Da Nang for the operation area, and, finally, the men of this new class of ship wanted, and deserved, a chance to prove her worth. At least two fast patrol boats (PCPs), known as Swift boats, also would be desirable. The over-and-under .50-caliber machine gun/81-mm. mortar mounted on the fantail of these boats is a formidable weapon, especially when the mortar is fired in the direct, trigger-fired mode. The Swifts would have to be selected from those on patrol on either side of the trawler's track when the time came. When the planners secured, the trawler was still heading nearly along her D.R. track toward Cape Batangan. Next morning, they were delighted to learn that she was still on track.

It now became necessary to make sure that no Market Time units got in the way of the trawler to scare her off again. The patrol aircraft were called off, leaving the tracking job completely to the *Wilhoite*. Word went out to all Market Time and Republic of Vietnam Navy units in the southern I Corps area that a trawler was headed toward the beach and to stay clear of her unless ordered to engage. The commanding generals, of the III Marine Amphibious Force, the Second Brigade of the Republic of Korea Marine Corps, and the U.S. Army's Task Force Oregon, at Chu Lai were advised that a trawler was being tracked by Market Time units and might possibly beach in one of their tactical areas of responsibilities (TAORs). Security forces on the beach would be required.

The NSG plan called for grouping the ships astern of the trawler in such a way that she could turn neither left or right to escape, but would have to continue toward the beach.

At noon, the First Coastal Zone Psychological Operations Officer, Lieutenant "Pete" Reiling, recommended to the Task Group Commander that a PsyOps speaker-team be included in the operation to try to talk the trawler into surrendering.* He argued that the speaker team would also come in handy if the operation ever reached the boarding phase. Obviously, however, a 50-foot Swift boat would be too crowded to carry the

---

* See V. G. Reiling, Jr., and G. W. Scott, "Psychological Operations in Vietnam," U.S. Naval Institute *Proceedings*, July 1968, pp. 122–134.

speaker equipment and the four members of the team. It would be impossible to fight the boat with so much excess cargo on board. It would also be next to impossible to "daisy chain," by way of patrol boats, all that gear and people down to the Quang Ngai area from Da Nang and expect it to be working when it got there. Even if they flew to Chu Lai and "daisy-chained" the rest of the way, it would be difficult. Too, whichever boat carried the speaker team would be in greater danger because she might have to close the trawler much nearer than any of the other units.

Pete countered these potential problems by suggesting that he and his team board a Market Time Coast Guard cutter (WPB) in Da Nang for the operation. The decision was made that if one of the cutters wanted to volunteer for the job, the speaker team could go. Pete departed to get his crew and gear ready, in the confident awareness that all the Coast Guard units in port would volunteer for the mission.

A short talk with the Commander Coast Guard Division 12 verified Pete's assurance, and the task of selecting the cutter for the job was quickly completed because the *Point Orient* (USCGC 82319) was just completing upkeep and was scheduled to go north on patrol the next day. Her commanding officer was briefed on how the speakers were to be used initially to challenge the trawler. The trawler's first inkling of enemy presence must be the spoken message requesting her to surrender. In the dark, it would be impossible for the trawler to take accurate aim on the sound source if her captain should decide to shoot at the WPB. If there was no reaction from the trawler after an appropriate period of repeating the taped message, the cutter was to fire illumination mortar rounds, still without giving the trawler a light source at which to take aim. If this did not bring a reaction from the trawler, the Swift and the cutter were to fire warning shots across her bow. If, after that, she continued to steam for the beach or attempted to evade her pursuers, she would be taken under fire.

The Psychological Operation team boarded the *Point Orient* just before she got underway at 1545 with orders to take station just south of

Cu Lao Re Island, east of Chu Lai, to await the procession as it passed by headed for the beach.

At 1300, the EOD man arrived as requested. By that time it appeared that getting underway at 1700 in the *Gallup* would permit a rendezvous with the *Wilhoite* at dusk. During the afternoon, plans were smoothed up; station assignments for the units were encrypted for transmission later. Since there is always the danger of two trawlers trying to infiltrate simultaneously, all units were advised to be particularly alert. The southernmost Swifts were placed on a special barrier. The *Wilhoite* was ordered to move out onto the starboard bow of the trawler, still at covert range, in order to expedite the rendezvous that was scheduled later that evening.

During the afternoon, orders arrived from the Task Force Commander to initiate challenge procedures when the trawler was five miles from the beach. Later he sent a message stating that the trawler had been positively identified—from the pictures taken by VP-1, plane No. 7—as a North Vietnamese resupply ship.

At 1715, the *Gallup* got underway, shifting to turbine power as soon as she had passed the deep water piers.

About an hour later, the *Gallup* passed the *Point Orient*. In order for the PsyOps team to test the range of their speaker system, the *Gallup* slowed down to about 20 knots and listened. An appropriate message had been taped after they had gotten underway and not only was it audible at 20 knots, but also it still could be heard when the *Gallup* went back up to 38 knots and resumed course to rendezvous with the *Wilhoite*.

At 2000, just after dark, the two ships met and the transfer was effected. The *Wilhoite's* captain had prepared his ship completely for boarding and hand-to-hand combat so that, if necessary, his ship could have tackled the entire job alone. The *Wilhoite* was ordered to take station five miles on the trawler's starboard quarter and the *Gallup* was ordered to make the long end-around run to get to the same position on the port quarter. The *Gallup,* using her turbine power, reached that position without delay.

At this time, the three ships were 22 miles east southeast of Cu Lao Re Island. The loom of the 12-mile light on the island was clearly visible. This powerful beacon is the main navigational aid in I Corps. Both the March and July trawlers undoubtedly had made landfall on it from far out at sea. The *Wilhoite's* CIC was tracking the trawler, the *Gallup* and the minesweeper *Pledge* (MSO-492)—which had moved to the southern barrier when the *Wilhoite* had begun her marathon tracking exercise— an LST headed north through the area ahead of the formation, plus a few other contacts. CIC was running the tactical and geographic plot on a second DRT. On this plot, a line had been drawn outlining the 12-mile contiguous area along the coast of the Republic of Vietnam. To this plot was added a five-mile zone off the beach to define the area where the PsyOps challenges would start.

All eyes were on the LST which was passing through the area, headed north. Would the trawler shy away from her, thinking her to be a patrol unit? The lookouts reported that the LST was well lighted, so perhaps the trawler would recognize her for what she was, a transiting ship. To the south of the LST was the *Pledge*. Her commander requested permission to investigate a stationary contact just south of Cu Lao Re Island. Since he would have had to cross in front of the trawler formation, it was necessary to deny permission. Besides, he might be needed on the southern barrier to interdict a possible second trawler. Also anticipating possible contact with the trawler, the *Pledge* had been fully prepared for action. She, too, was completely ready to tackle the job single-handedly.

The U.S. destroyer *Walker* (DP-517), was on her night gunfire support station, just off the entrance to Song Tra Khuc, the river which enters Quang Ngai city, and about three miles south of the Sa Ky River, at the base of Cape Batangan—in a position to ruin the whole ambush at the last minute. CSC advised her of what was happening and asked her to move out of the way. By that time, she held our formation on radar and graciously moved south out of the way to stand by if needed.

At 2130, a second contact showed south of Cu Lao Re and became dead in the water. A few minutes later, the *Point Orient* reported at rendezvous point, at the location of this second contact.

The trawler decreased speed to eight knots. She was reacting to the passing LST. The LST passed about eight miles in front of the trawler, proceeding innocently north to Chu Lai. The trawler went back up to ten knots when the LST had passed.

During the hour from 2130 until 2230, the trawler made one or two slight course changes, one of which took her a little farther south of Cu Lao Re than had her initial track, but then she steadied down on a westerly course headed directly for the coastline south of Cape Bantangan. Shortly thereafter, a message was received from the Task Force Commander, advising that a VC "Reception Committee" was waiting just up the Sa Ky river on its northern shore to offload the trawler. This bit of intelligence clinched the trawler's destination. Now it would be possible to select the Swift boat which would be closest to the track of the trawler, and therefore the one which was needed to fill the port quarter slot in the formation, since the *Point Orient* was scheduled to take the starboard quarter position. It was the *PCF-79*.

So, with all ships selected, at 2230 the encrypted station assignments were sent out, to be executed later on signal.

The trawler was now 25 miles from the beach. The *Point Orient* was still sitting up there south of Cu Lao Re, about nine miles north of the formation's track. Since the trawler's best speed was estimated at 15 knots and since the *Point Orient's* was only a few more than that, it became apparent that the cutter should begin taking station if she was to avoid a long stern chase. For this reason she was ordered to take station astern of the trawler at 3,000 yards, staying at least three miles from the trawler until aft of her beam. The *Wilhoite* and the *Gallup* were ordered to close to three miles.

After that, they just steamed, watching the trawler get closer and closer to that 12-mile line. Because it might be crucial should the trawler decide to turn away, the line was plotted again, more accurately. Excitement built up rapidly within the quiet, darkened CIC as the trawler was plotted closer and closer to the line. She steamed over the line and onward with no hesitation. At that time, 2330, all units were ordered to preassigned stations. The *Wilhoite* took station 20 degrees abaft the starboard beam of the trawler at 5,000 yards, the *Gallup* a similar station aft the port beam. The *Orient* and the *PCF-79* proceeded to stations on the starboard and port quarters respectively at 2,500 yards. All units went to General Quarters.

The Task Force Commander directed that suppressive fire be employed around the area in case the trawler beached. CSC suggested that gunfire support be arranged with the *Walker*. The Swift boat Division Commander (COMCOSDIV 16) at Chu Lai volunteered helo gunships from Task Force Oregon to disperse the Reception Committee. He was asked to have the gunships standing by on call, since the On Scene Commander felt that he could control them more effectively than the several other varieties of supporting arms which were available.

The *PCF-79* closed at high speed from the west, circling astern of the *Gallup* to get to station. She was still about 1,000 yards from station, boring in at full speed when the trawler crossed the five-mile line from the beach. It was 11 minutes after midnight, 15 July. The quarter moon was low in the west and had gone behind heavy clouds. The *Point Orient* was standing by to commence the tape broadcast. On order, the Vietnamese language broadcast began: "You must stop and don't shoot because you are surrounded! We knew clearly that you were coming here and we have been waiting for you for three days. You must quickly wake up to the fact and surrender. The government will be merciful."

The message was repeated again and again as the *Orient* closed to a range of 1,000 yards. The spoken challenge was to be used for five minutes before taking the next step. After his tape had been played several times, a Vietnamese Navy PsyOps Officer took the microphone and began pleading with the crew of the trawler to surrender. Earlier in the afternoon when Pete had asked this officer to come along "to help try to capture a trawler" he had reacted with a great deal of skepticism—not for the plan, but at the thought that we knew there was a trawler out there to be captured. During that afternoon and evening, as the tapes were prepared, his skepticism gave way to belief and then incredulity. When he saw the trawler on radar, his excitement was almost beyond containing. Imagine, then, his excitement—and everyone else's—when, at 0016, the *Orient* fired her first 81-mm. illumination round and there, big as life, before our eyes was the enemy trawler.

The *PCF-79* reached a mortar-firing position and began illuminating also, so that the trawler had continuous illumination during the next phase of the operation. After five full minutes of illumination and ten minutes of PsyOps, the *Orient* and the *PCF-79* were ordered to commence firing .50-caliber tracers across the infiltrator's bow. The silence and black of the night were shattered by the noise as the red points of light formed a tight V in front of the trawler. Still, she made no attempt to slow down, stop, reply to the challenges, or do anything but bore onward toward the entrance to the Sa Ky River. After two or three minutes of warning fire, the *PCF-79's* skipper reported "He's trying to escape up the river. Request permission to take him under fire." All criteria had been met to establish the trawler as the enemy and as an evading, hostile unit, even though she had not yet opened fire on the task unit. Permission was granted to commence firing. A call went out for the gunships from Task Force Oregon. The two small craft opened up immediately with an intense fire from their six .50-caliber machine guns and two mortars. The *Gallup* commenced fire with 3-inch VT frag—to suppress topside personnel on the trawler—and with her 40-mm. guns. The *Wilhoite* had to maneuver to avoid shallow water, then joined with her 3-inch and 40-mm. weapons. At about 0038, the *PCF-79* closed to 200 yards and fired a white phosphorus mortar round into the pilothouse of the trawler. A couple of minutes later, out of control, she grounded in the river mouth. While both of our small craft paused to reload machine guns, the trawler opened up on them with fire from her 12.7-mm. deck guns. Three rounds of 57-mm. recoilless were fired in the direction of the Swift boat. Both craft returned fire and suppressed the fire coming from the trawler. A high explosive mortar round went off in the pilothouse, followed by explosions of other mortar rounds fired into the superstructure of the trawler by the two units. The explosion blew out the starboard side pilothouse door, pinning down and killing one crew member who had been firing an AK-56.

A Task Force Oregon flare ship and two helo gunships arrived on station about the time the trawler grounded. They requested, and got, permission to join in the attack. The flare ship took over illumination responsibilities, while the gunships' rockets and red fingers of M-60 fire clawed across the trawler from one side to the other. All other units continued firing. The trawler had turned starboard side to her attackers after grounding. Fire from all units was effective and the trawler appeared to be burning from one end to the other.

The helo gunships were relieved on station by two others and the attack continued virtually unabated until 0115 when one of the advisors with the Korean Marine Corps called to announce that the ROKs were going to commence bombarding the area with their artillery to suppress any of the Reception Committee who might still be around. Since the seaborne units were on the extension of the Koreans' gun target line, they had to move south out of the way. This resulted in their being far enough away that their fire was much less effective. For perhaps an hour the Korean artillery rounds fell fairly frequently. At about two o'clock, the destroyer *Walker* was also assigned a fire mission in the area of the trawler.

So, for several hours, rounds fell around and on the trawler from many directions. About 0315, it became necessary to think about detaching the *Point Orient* and sending her back to Da Nang to go on her assigned patrol. She would have to rearm, her skipper reported, and he estimated that his ammo would be depleted in about five minutes. As the *Orient* completed firing, a relief for her was requested from COMCOSDIV 16.

At 0320, the *Point Orient* departed for Da Nang, having spent the preceding hour in close to the trawler, firing slowly, deliberately and quite accurately. At 0330, the *PCF-20* arrived from the next Market Time station north to relieve the *Orient*. At 0415, the *PCF-79* expended all her ammo and returned to Chu Lai, being replaced at 0430 by the *PCF-54*.

During the remainder of the night the five ships continued to illuminate the trawler and keep the fires on board burning. When, a little after 0430, the fires had almost completely died out, the two Swifts went in for close attacks, renewing the fires on board and brightening up the night again.

Dawn arrived at 0600 and full light by 0630 when the *Walker* started a called-fire mission in several landing areas where the Korean Marines would be bringing in their security troops. By 0700, three junks from Vietnamese Navy Coastal Group 16 near Quang Ngai and three junks from Coastal Group 15 at Chu Lai arrived. The On Scene Commander transferred from the *Wilhoite* to the *PCF-20* and, in company with the other Swifts and six junks, started in toward the trawler. The helos which were bringing the security forces began arriving in droves at two or three landing zones. When it appeared that there were adequate friendly forces around and no fire fights within earshot, the *PCF-20* approached the trawler. We were confident that the initial intense rain of fire from the sea and air units in the first few minutes after the ship grounded most certainly must have prevented the crew from staying around to arm the destructive system.

As we got near enough to read the bow numbers, I was stunned to read the number 441. I realized, however, that the North Vietnamese frequently change bow numbers to confuse our forces.

The water in the Sa Ky mouth is shallow and full of rocks. One huge flat rock that looks like a reddish brown lava cinder lies in the center of the river mouth. If the trawler had kept to the south of this rock, she might have been able to get into the river. As it was, however, the white phosphorus round which the *PCF-79* put into the pilothouse put the ship out of control and she grounded about 75 yards to the northeast of the flat rock. Due to the presence of the submerged rocks and shallow waters, the Swift was picking her way very carefully toward our prize. The junks, however, reached the trawler and the Vietnamese sailors boarded her. Three U.S. advisors were with them.

The trawler had grounded in the ROK Marine Corps TAOR, so they felt more than a slight proprietary interest in her. This being the case, they decided it would be well if we would leave. After putting the request in terms that would have been very difficult to refuse, we retreated from the trawler and lay off for the remainder of the morning, watching.

The trawler appeared to be floating, except for being caught at one point at the stern. She was rolling freely in the swell. It looked as if she might float if she were pulled off the sandbar. The Task Force Commander was contacted and permission was requested to try to salvage the trawler and take her back to Da Nang. He replied "Bring her home!" Soon thereafter the Korean Marines were officially requested to help "assist the Navy" to salvage the craft. This they were already hard at work doing—lightening her by removing all the weapons. When, late in the morning, all the weapons had been removed, U.S. Marine Corps CH-46 helos from Chu Lai flew in and landed on the big flat rock where the weapons had been stacked. They were loaded into the helos and flown off to the Second ROK Brigade Headquarters.

At 1300, responding to our request, the NSA detachment at Chu Lai sent two Mike boats (LCM-8s) to help salvage the ship. While the Mike boats were underway, the ROK Marines completed their work and left the ship to us to attempt to salvage. By this time, the Coastal Group 16 junks had returned to their base to fill an operational commitment, but the Coastal Group 15 junk men had remained to help.

During the morning the Vietnamese coastal minesweeper *MSC-115*, and the Vietnamese Gunboat *PGM-618* with their respective U.S. Navy advisors on board, had arrived and were standing by to help. The water, however, was too shallow for any but the junks. Having transferred to the

Coastal Group 15 Command Junk, we proceeded to board the trawler. As we neared her, a little smoke was still coming out of the vents that came from the living spaces in the after superstructure. The *Pledge* had volunteered to do the entire salvage job, but it was felt that the units of more shallow draft should try first.

It was expected that the holds would be empty when we arrived on board. Yet, incredibly, all the ammunition—amounting to many tons— was still there. The EOD man set to work immediately looking for demolition charges in the holds. He found them and disarmed them. The starboard bow numbers were checked and sure enough, there was a removable plate inserted in a holder on the bow. On the port side the plate was missing so there was no number at all. It was a surprise to pull out the starboard side plate and, instead of finding 459 painted on the back side; find, instead 418. After examining the 441 side more carefully it was clear that the number 59 had been washed with paint remover and painted over to read 441. The remains of other numbers could actually be read under the 59 if one looked carefully. Later, the port side bow number plate was found in the boatswain's locker under the forecastle. It read 459 on one side and 418 on the other. The 59 had not yet been repainted to read 41.

Topside, the trawler was a shambles. The entire stern superstructure was burned out and riddled with bullet holes of assorted sizes. The contents of the living spaces on the main deck and the pilothouse on the 01 deck had been reduced to a grey powder. The starboard side gunwales were ripped and torn. Six large-caliber holes were found in the starboard side and hundreds of smaller ones.

Fishing nets, floats, and even artificial wooden fish were strewn about the decks, in a confused mess with tarps which had covered the holds, the hatch cover battens, fire hoses, and much more paraphernalia.

Despite her blazing appearance during the night, only the after section of the trawler had been burned. The paint forward had not even been blistered. The ammunition ready box, between the engine room skylights and the after hold was wooden, covered with canvas. The canvas was burned and the wood scorched, but the contents had not burned. Inside were many cans of belted 12.7-mm. ammo, and several 57-mm. recoilless rounds.

Expended and exploded 12.7-mm. brass lay around the deck in profusion. Two exploded 5-gallon "jerry" cans lay near the engine room skylight. Almost the only identifiable thing in the pilothouse was a hand-thrown antitank grenade which was obviously there to be used to repel boarders.

The after 12.7-mm. gun on the 01 deck had been fired extensively.

The ship seemed to be aground either on the screw or the rudder. Most of the hull floated on the crest of each wave so that it rolled back and forth, the bilge-keel of each side bumping on the bottom with the passage of each wave.

Getting around the deck was very hazardous. Carrying a weapon was even more difficult. I put my M-14 on the Command Junk where it would be safe. I was soon to regret this action.

There were now six of us, four Americans, and two South Vietnamese, on the trawler. An attempt to pull the trawler free had failed when the lines from the Command Junk parted. There was nothing to do but wait for them to get more line from the *PGM-618* and the Swift boats. On the big flat rock were the Korean Marines who had not yet been helo-lifted out. We also knew that there were still security forces in the hills surrounding the river mouth. We were not alone—yet—although the security forces were due to leave at 1600. We spent the next half-hour in going over the boat thoroughly for familiarization and for intelligence purposes. The holds were in good condition, although there were several 50-caliber holes in the after hold near the waterline, which leaked each time the ship rolled to starboard.

About 1400, we began to wonder when the junk was coming back. Looking seaward, the junk could be seen moving from one unit to another. Looking was about all there was to do. We had done everything possible until we could get something to pull on the ship. About that time, all hands on board discovered that they were thirsty, but there was no water in the trawler—our canteens were in the Command Junk. Also, there were radios on the Command Junk with which we could have communicated to the Swifts and the other units. I then realized that most of our weapons were on the junk.

We took stock of what weapons we had: one M-16 with extra ammo, and one hand weapon. We began to apprehend that we were somewhat isolated and not in a terribly comfortable position in case some sniper should sneak through the security forces. We learned quickly what every foot soldier knows instinctively: never get separated from your weapon. Suddenly, life on board a trawler—specifically, this one—seemed quite lonely.

But more pressing thoughts quickly dispelled our morbid speculations.

What, for example, would we do with the trawler when the security forces had to leave? It wouldn't be practical to leave a guard on her overnight. She would have to be illuminated all night to prevent the VC from boarding and removing the ammo. Destroying the trawler in case she couldn't be hauled off the sandbar had to be considered, also.

Preoccupation with these problems was interrupted when a helo landed on the flat rock and one of the several officers on board swam out to the trawler and climbed aboard. He was from the MACV Captured Materials Exploitation Company and had come to take a look at the ammunition. He was very excited about what we had. After a thorough inspection, he left. His reaction strengthened our resolve to salvage the ship if only for her valuable ammo.

A few minutes before 1500, the *PGM-618, MSC-115*, a Swift, and the junks all began moving in our general direction, obviously feeling their way very carefully. Apparently they had arrived at a plan of action and were on their way to try it out.

At 1500, two LCM-8s came around the point from Chu Lai and headed straight for us. What a welcome sight! The landing craft were not, however, an instant solution to the problem. The only water relatively clear of rocks led up to the starboard quarter of the trawler. The Mike boats were blocked from approaching the bow by the many rocks in the water. Therefore, the Mikes tried at first to pull the stern off the sandbar. The boats pulled, but instead of pulling straight out of starboard, they pulled at a safer angle of about 135 degrees. This caused the trawler to slip aft and become more firmly grounded on the sandbar. After nearly an hour and several more abortive attempts, the lines were walked up to the bow to attempt a new approach. While all this was going on, the helos had arrived for the Koreans and the last of them disappeared over the horizon a few minutes after 1600. The Mike-boat crews were told, "There isn't anyone left here now but us and the VC, so you'd better get us out of here pretty quick." Thus encouraged, the skipper of the LCM-8 boat, No. 852 took a heavy strain on the two lines from the bow, headed out on a slightly hazardous course, jammed the throttles to the bulkhead, and pulled. The bow started to swing, the trawler pivoting on her grounded point aft. Faster and faster she swung through the 135 degrees necessary to get her headed for open water. The Mike boat continued to tow the ship out farther and farther into good water. When about half a mile off the beach, she stopped, and each LCM made up alongside one side of the trawler. A stop at Chu Lai to have the holes patched was obviously necessary before continuing the longer trip to Da Nang. Thus, at 1630, LCM-8 boats, No. 852 and No. 798, started off at best speed for Chu Lai, the trawler tied securely between them.

At about 1700, our EOD man GMG2 Eddie Knaup, who was on board the trawler, noticed that she was no longer emitting puffs of ash and smoke from her vents, but instead was smoking hard. He entered the main deck living spaces and saw heavy smoke pouring out of a hatch which went down to a storeroom under the main deck. He knew that one of the largest demolition charges was in that storeroom. He lifted the hatch cover carefully and saw fire playing around the TNT in the storeroom. He dropped the hatch cover, and ran across the starboard LCM to a Swift boat which was made up and towing outboard of the

LCM, yelling to the LCMs to stop in order to eliminate the high relative wind which was sweeping through the trawler, fanning the fires. He led out a hose from the Swift boat, across the LCM and then entered the compartment again, opened the hatch and stood there spraying water on the fire. By the light of the flames he could clearly see that the primacord wound around the center block of TNT was smoldering and might ignite at any instant. Still, he stood his ground and fought the fire. Meanwhile the Swift boat had called in the *PCF-79*, which tied up outboard of the port side LCM and led over a second fire hose. With this one, they soon had the fire under control and then extinguished. They checked thoroughly for any other sparks or smoldering fires before resuming the trip to Chu Lai.

At 2030, the trawler was tied up at the pier side at Naval Support Activity Da Nang Detachment, Chu Lai. A security watch was posted on board to keep off the curious and the souvenir hunters.

At 0430 in the morning of the 16th, the trawler settled stern first in the water alongside the pier, although the bow remained afloat. The water used to fight the fire had increased the draft so that the many small bullet holes near the waterline were now below the waterline. These holes permitted the slow intake of water, eventually sinking the stern.

This complication added considerably to the problem of handling the trawler. It had been intended to off-load her completely that morning, but not with the after hold full of water. She would have to be off-loaded and salvaged at the same time.

The support forces at Chu Lai did a magnificent job, and she was empty and afloat before noon. The holes were patched and she was ready to be picked up at the sea buoy next morning by the Vietnamese *PGM-618*.

On Monday, the 17th, the trawler transited to the Da Nang Naval Base of the Vietnamese Navy. That same day the Koreans turned over some of the weapons to the Vietnamese Navy. Others were delivered the following day—nearly a thousand in all. The trawler had carried over

1,600 weapons, some estimates ranged as high as 3,000—arms and ammunition sufficient to supply a Viet Cong regiment for several months, 90 tons in all.

One now hears this engagement variously referred to as "that trawler the ROKs captured" or "the Navy's VC trawler," or "that trawler the Huey's beached at Batangan."

The Sa Ky River Victory, as it is now referred to by the Vietnamese, is all of those things and more, because that battered hulk represents a victory of the combined Allied arms. The lion's share of the credit, however, belongs to the Operation Market Time Forces, who fulfilled their mission so professionally and admirably. But, a special word of praise is in order for the *Pledge,* and those Swift boats which patrolled within eye and earshot of the action, and, overcoming with exemplary discipline, an almost irrepressible urge to join the battle, maintained the integrity of their patrols. They also serve. . . .

A graduate of Illinois Institute of Technology in 1952, **Commander Stephan** had risen to ET1 during his enlisted service from 1942 to 1948. He has served in the USS *Mississippi* (BAG-128), the destroyers *Shields* (DD-596) and *Lyman K. Swenson* (DD-729), and has commanded the USS *Tom Green County* (LST-1159). During separate tours of duty, from 1957 to 1960, and from 1964 to 1966, he participated in development and production of Fire Control and Guidance Systems for the FBM System, and Polaris Command and Control Communications. He was Senior Naval Advisor to the Vietnamese Navy in I Corps, and Commander, Northern Surveillance Group (CTG-115.1) before assuming command of the USS *Duncan* (DDR-874) in March 1968.

"God Be Here"

7

Lieutenant Commander Thomas J. Cutler, USN

U.S. Naval Institute *Proceedings*
(April 1988): 79–83

THE LIEUTENANT PULLED OFF his black beret and threw it down on top of the PBR's grenade locker. The black loop of ribbon at the back of the beret had been cut into two pennants—among PBR sailors this signified that he had made his first contact with the enemy—and the ends of each pennant were notched with a V to represent his first enemy kill. Both ceremonial cuts had been made a long time ago. The lieutenant had tallied several hundred patrols since joining River Section 511, and he had engaged the enemy in more than 60 firefights. Back in his locker in Binh Thuy, under a pile of neatly folded olive-drab undershirts, was a Purple Heart he had earned last November when a piece of shrapnel lodged in his jaw. He had had a PBR shot out from under him as well, and he and his crew had been raked by intense small-arms fire at close range while they swam for their lives. . . .

Despite all the action that the lieutenant had seen, the enlisted men in River Section 511 liked to have him along as patrol officer on their patrols. He was a "cool head" in combat, and as a "mustang"—an enlisted man who had worked his way up through the ranks—he knew what enlisted men were all about and how to look out for them. There was another reason they liked having him as patrol officer. Sailors are by nature superstitious, and men in combat are often more religious than they were back home. So the sailors liked having the lieutenant along because his name was Dick Godbehere, pronounced exactly as spelled: God-be-here! It was not uncommon to hear someone say, in a play on words that had a measure of seriousness, "I'd rather have Godbehere than anyone else."

The year was 1968, two days before the start of the Vietnamese holiday called Tet. Lieutenant Godbehere's patrol had been assigned a psychological operations mission, one designed to get information to villagers about the government and the war effort. The PBRs were good vehicles for these missions because they could get close to the people in the delta by traveling the rivers and canals. Godbehere's PBR was rigged with a tape recorder and large speakers to broadcast their message, an appeal for the South Vietnamese Government's *Chieu Hoi* (open arms) program—the amnesty program that promised protection, money, clothes, and food for any VC who wished to change sides. A sign on each side of the PBR said in Vietnamese, "This is a *Chieu Hoi* Rally Point. You will be welcomed here." Godbehere looked at the sign and wondered if any ralliers (called *Hoi Chanhs)* would turn themselves in to him that day. That had happened to other PBRs on patrol, but so far never to Godbehere. He had read a report somewhere that said 28,000 *Hoi Chanhs* had rallied in the previous year. He had also read that the estimated cost of the *Chieu Hoi* program was about $150 per *Hoi Chanh*—compared to the unofficial estimate of $9,000 worth of ammunition expended per enemy killed.

The two-boat patrol got under way and headed down the Bassac River toward the major delta city of Can Tho. Godbehere disliked psychological operations patrols because the PBRs had to move slowly in order to allow the messages to be heard, which made them very vulnerable to attack, and because listening to the taped messages over and over challenged his sanity.

After about 20 minutes, the tape recorder was switched on and the crew settled in for what promised to be a boring patrol. The pre-mission brief had predicted a quiet run. Just a few weeks back, General William Desobry, U.S. Army, upon being relieved as U.S. military advisory chief in the delta region, told reporters that the Viet Cong were "poorly motivated, poorly trained" and that the South Vietnamese Army "has the upper hand completely." The area around Can Tho was considered relatively friendly.

But as they plodded along, Godbehere had been scanning the banks, and the hair at the back of his neck was beginning to prickle. He had seen the grass-covered huts along the banks with chickens clucking and strutting in front. Tools rested against thatched walls and fishnets were piled or strewn about. An occasional water buffalo would swing its massive horned head in their direction to detect the source of noise as they passed, and the grunting of pigs could sometimes be heard over the rumble of the engines. Rice baskets swayed on hooks in the breeze and hints of incense tickled the nostrils every now and then. It was a pastoral scene except for one element: not a single human being had been in sight for the last several miles. Godbehere had been around long enough to know that this usually spelled trouble.

"I don't like the looks of this, Boats," he said to the boat captain.

"I know, sir. Too quiet," came the reply. The boat captain had one hand resting lightly on the reined-in throttles. "Gunner, get your helmet on," he called forward to the third-class petty officer lounging in the gun tub.

The rest of the crew fastened their flak jackets and warily watched the banks.

Godbehere said to no one in particular, "Charlie's out there. I can feel him."

Seconds crept into minutes as perspiration flowed down tense brows into anxious eyes. The minutes grew into hours that seemed like days as they droned along, the taped Vietnamese voice appealing to unseen ears. Twenty-eight miles passed and nothing happened, yet the tension remained. Something was unquestionably wrong.

As they turned about for the return trip, the boat captain said, "Maybe it's got something to do with this Tet holiday thing. Maybe that's why nobody's around."

"Maybe," Godbehere said, not believing it.

The return trip was more of the same. Everything looked normal in the villages except for the absence of the people. The Americans passed from hamlet to hamlet feeling as if they were the only humans left in the world. Only the infrequent passage of a plane or the distant *whop-whop* of helicopter blades occasionally dispelled this sensation. Godbehere couldn't shake the feeling of being watched, of believing that at any moment all hell would break loose.

But it never did. The patrol ended at last, and Godbehere and the others returned to base trying to work the knots of tension out of their muscles. They were exhausted.

That night after Godbehere had filed his patrol report and turned in, he lay under his green mosquito net watching the geckos patrolling the walls of his hootch in search of insect prey. He wondered what the strange day meant. The signs were there for trouble—the situation had "ambush" written all over it. And the PBRs were so vulnerable at the low speed required by the mission—Charlie could have hit them if it had in fact been an ambush. But he didn't. Why? Maybe the boat captain was right: maybe it had something to do with Tet. Maybe the villagers had all gone to their temples or something . . . No, the animals wouldn't have been left to wander and the tools would have been put away. There were people nearby; he was sure of it . . . But why were they hiding? If Charlie was there, why hadn't he ambushed the PBRs? . . .

Godbehere mulled over these possibilities for a long time before he was able to go to sleep.

Two days later, Dick Godbehere had his answers. The enemy had chosen the Tet holiday of 1968 to launch a coordinated, country-wide offensive within South Vietnam. Thirty-six of the 44 provincial capitals, five of the six major cities, and many district capitals and hamlets were attacked by communist forces. In the Mekong Delta, the attacks involved 13 of the 16 provincial capitals, including Can Tho, the city near which Godbehere's patrol had been. Four days before Tet, the enemy troops had moved into the hamlets around Can Tho in preparation for the assault. Godbehere had been right: Charlie was there when the PBRs had come through. He had apparently refrained from attacking the small game of two PBRs in order not to reveal his presence before the large-scale attack on Can Tho scheduled to begin in unison with the other attacks throughout the country on the first day of Tet.

The battles of the Tet Offensive raged for 77 days. Game Warden units played a significant role in reversing the tide of battle in the delta. By chance, some units happened to be in the vicinity of the city of Chau Doc, involved in a planned interdiction operation called "Bold Dragon I," when the Tet Offensive began. These few Game Warden sailors and the SEALs on the operation with them played a major role in the defense of the city. The VC battalions assigned to capture Chau Doc, told that they would be met with waving banners and open arms, were quite surprised when met by the resistance led by the Game Warden sailors. PBRs and Seawolf helicopters also provided the firepower that held the enemy at bay in Ben Tre until reinforcing ground troops could arrive to drive the attackers out of the city.

During February, Lieutenant Godbehere was involved in a few skirmishes on the periphery of the major battles, but nothing terribly significant. This proved to be a lull before the storm for Dick Godbehere.

Lieutenant Godbehere's two-PBR patrol left Binh Thuy and headed southeast on the Bassac River en route to its assigned patrol area. The sky was growing dark, and the air was cool for a March night in the Mekong Delta.

Signalman Third Class Jere Beery, the after gunner on the PBR carrying Godbehere, politely looked away as one of the other crew members squatted over the rail of the boat, paying the price for having indulged in a local village's culinary delights. Privacy is one of the casualties of war—particularly on a 31-foot boat with no head.

Beery looked down at his own tailor-made camouflage uniform, but the sky was too dark for him to really see it. He had just bought the outfit from a local Vietnamese seamstress and was wearing it for the first time. His shipmates had teased him about it, saying, "Hey, Jere, where are you? I can't see you with those camis on," or "Look at the walking tree."

The PBRs passed by Can Tho. Most of the city was quiet and dark, but the distant rattle of a machine gun could be heard from the far side. Some weeks back, Can Tho had been enveloped in artillery fire and exploding aircraft ordnance as the allied forces fought to dislodge the Viet Cong from the university there. Beery had heard that the once beautiful Faculty of Science building had been reduced to smoking rubble, but he hadn't seen it.

A reporter who had come along for a story bumped into something in the dark and cursed the offending object and its ancestry. Beery remembered another occasion when a pair of reporters had talked Beery's boat captain into taking them into an infamous area known as the Ti Ti Canal. One of the pair was a large-framed man, wearing brand-new fatigues, who had told the section's commanding officer, "We need to show the people back in the States exactly what our boys are going through over here." The other was a man about half his companion's size. They had lugged several cases of camera equipment on board for the patrol. On the way to the canal, the big man was standing on the engine covers with his 16-mm. motion-picture camera on top of the boat's awning. As they neared the canal, Bailey, the boat captain, had hollered back to Beery, "Tell that son-of-a-bitch to get down here and put on a flak jacket and helmet." Beery relayed the message (in more polite terms), only to be rebuffed. "I can't maneuver the camera with all that stuff on," the big reporter had said. No sooner had he uttered those words than automatic-weapons fire erupted from both banks. The 16-mm. camera flew up into the air as the big reporter dove into the coxswain's flat, landing right at Bailey's feet. The boat captain kicked the reporter and yelled, "You better get up there and get your pictures, you son-of-a-bitch, we ain't comin' through here for you again!" The reporter's camera had been broken, and the only things to show for their efforts were a few still photographs taken by the little reporter and 136 bullet-entry holes in the hull of the PBR. The two PBRs passed the upriver end of Cu Lao Mae Island. It was totally black on the river now. Only the radar could see.

A sudden flash of light appeared in Beery's peripheral vision over his left shoulder. He turned and realized that it must have been a BAD rocket, for a second one had just emerged from the darkness of the island. Both rockets were well off target.

Beery could hear Lieutenant Godbehere on the radio—"Red Rose, this is Hand Lash Delta"—checking to make sure there were no friendly units in the area. All gunners were holding their fire, not only because of the possibility of friendly units but because the flashes from their weapons would give Charlie something besides sound to aim at.

Godbehere got the clearance he sought from "Red Rose" and ordered his patrol units to start a firing run. The PBRs swooped in toward the island and hammered the darkness from which the rockets had come. Flames of small-arms fire and machine-gun bursts flickered in the trees on shore as the boats roared in.

Beery squeezed off about a hundred rounds and then leaned down to open another canister of ammunition. Two fireballs burst out of the trees as he bent over. Beery recognized them as B-40 rounds but was certain that they would miss. He was wrong: one of the rockets struck the gunwale on the starboard quarter and exploded.

Lieutenant Godbehere was just aft of the coxswain's flat when the rocket hit. As he saw the reddish-orange rocket explode, he felt a blast of heat and pieces of shrapnel tearing into his legs. A few moments later a second rocket found its mark, this one detonating against the grenade locker on the starboard side. Godbehere, thrown to the deck by the blast, climbed back to his feet and looked about, trying to assess his situation. A gunner named Sherman had been standing near Godbehere before the hits; now he was gone. Godbehere thought he had been blown overboard, but soon he appeared next to the lieutenant, a steel fragment protruding from the back of his arm and another lodged in his foot. Aft,

Godbehere saw that Beery was still standing at his gun but wasn't firing. "Go see what's wrong with Beery," Godbehere told Sherman and then turned his attention back to the battle that was still raging.

The other PBR in the patrol had been hit many times, and the damage to both boats was too severe to warrant any further engagement. Godbehere ordered the boat captains to retire to a safe location so that they could evacuate their wounded.

Sherman reappeared and said, "Beery's hurt bad, Mr. Godbehere."

Godbehere moved aft. Every step was painful; clearly, his legs had taken a lot of metal. When he got to Beery, the young gunner was still standing and holding on to his weapon. "Where're you hit?" Godbehere asked.

"In the gut," Beery rasped.

Godbehere looked down. To his dismay and horror, he saw that Beery's abdomen had been sliced open by the exploding rocket: his intestines were trailing down to a grisly heap on the PBR's deck.

Godbehere grasped Beery firmly by the shoulders and, with Sherman's help, laid him down on the deck, then carefully piled the moist entrails onto Beery's abdomen. With a large battle dressing he cautiously covered the hideous mound. Sherman cut away Beery's trousers; the new camis were full of shrapnel holes, and his right leg and hip were a mess. A large piece of shrapnel had penetrated Beery's stomach and was protruding from his back. Godbehere doubted that Beery was going to live.

While Godbehere and Sherman worked, trying to dress Beery's many wounds, Beery tried to speak but didn't have sufficient breath left to be heard above the PBR's engines. He pulled Godbehere down and whispered in his ear. "If I don't make it," he said so softly that Godbehere could barely hear him, "tell my mom and dad what happened."

Godbehere said, "You're going to be all right. Your intestines just fell out. They can put 'em back for you. They do it all the time. You'll be okay."

Beery shook his head slowly.

Godbehere yelled, "Goddammit, Jere, you're going to be all right!"

The two PBRs were out of the firefight by this time, and Godbehere ordered them to head for Tra On village on the east bank of the Bassac River opposite Cu Lao Mae Island. Godbehere had visited several of the eight U.S. Army advisors there, and he knew the village pretty well. It was the nearest place he could think of to effect a safe medical evacuation. As the two boats headed downriver toward Tra On, Godbehere told Bailey to get on the radio and call for "Pedro," the Air Force medical evacuation helicopter. For the rest of the run into Tra On, Godbehere knelt next to Beery in a pool of their mingled blood, ignoring his own wounds and trying to soothe the mangled man's fear and despair.

At the village, the Army advisors loaded Beery onto a stretcher. As they started to carry him off the boat, Beery smiled weakly and said, "I don't know how those guys managed to hit me." He held up a tattered remnant of his brand-new camouflage shirt. "I thought I looked like a tree."

Neither Lieutenant Godbehere nor Petty Officer Beery ever fought in Vietnam again. Dick Godbehere's wounds were serious enough to cause his evacuation for recovery and reassignment. He eventually retired from the Navy as a lieutenant commander.

The same spirit that had permitted Jere Beery to make a joke about his camouflage uniform in his hour of crisis got him through a long and trying ordeal of recovery. He lived and went on to become a motion-picture stunt man.

Commander Cutler served as an in-country naval advisor to South Vietnamese forces from January to December 1972, taking part in numerous river and harbor patrols, coastal surveillance operations, and Vietnamization projects. He also served on the staff of the U.S. naval advisory group in Saigon. He now teaches history at the U.S. Naval Academy and writes the monthly "Books of Interest" column for *Proceedings*.

8 "Seawolves Roll In across the Mekong Delta"

Commander David G. Tyler, USNR

U.S. Naval Institute *Proceedings*
(January 2002): 45–49

The labyrinth of rivers spilling onto the coastal flats of South Vietnam was a supply highway for the Vietcong. Mustered to curtail this traffic were U.S. Navy river patrol boats. But their vulnerability to enemy ambush called for support from the air: "Scramble Seawolves!"

A NEW DIMENSION in naval aviation burst forth in South Vietnam in 1967. To fight an enemy with an extensive coastline and intricate system of inland waterways and to transform its antisubmarine warfare and search-and-rescue way of thinking, the Navy began to employ helicopters in direct-action missions against enemy ground forces. Those who were thrust into this underdeveloped method of warfare expanded and refined the tactical applications of maritime helicopter operations.

The Mekong Delta is a fertile agricultural region and consequently highly populated. In 1970 almost half the republic's people lived between the Bassac and My Tho rivers. More than 80% of South Vietnam's rice crop is grown in this region. The area is swampy and susceptible to flooding in monsoon season, making bridge building difficult, if not impossible. In fact, in many areas of the delta, marine transport is the only feasible mode of travel. More important, because of the overland distance from North Vietnam, equipping communist sympathizers in this region was done most efficiently from the sea.

In addition to stopping infiltration, the goal was to ensure safe passage of friendly shipping along inland waterways, especially the Long Tau River. The primary transportation route between Saigon and the South China Sea, this was a crucial thoroughfare for provisioning U.S. forces. The Vietcong (VC) thrived in this region—labeled the Rung Sat Special Zone by the Military Assistance Command, Vietnam—mining the narrow river and ambushing merchant vessels from densely forested riverbanks.

In 1964, North Vietnam intensified efforts to ship large volumes of small arms and munitions to guerrillas in the south. In February 1965 a vessel containing a large cache of weapons was discovered at Vung Ro Bay. Additional stockpiles found nearby solidified the belief that stronger measures were needed to halt the flow of arms to the VC. Army General William Westmoreland met with Vietnamese officials on 3 March 1965 to initiate a plan to cut off VC maritime supply lines. This became known as Operation Market Time and was assigned to Task Force (TF) 115.

The South Vietnamese Navy (VNN) was tasked to handle enemy junks intertwined with legitimate traffic traveling parallel to the coastline, and the U.S. Navy was to tackle enemy vessels of trawler size or larger that approached South Vietnam from offshore. The inland push by the U.S. Navy expanded rapidly with the establishment of Operation Game Warden in 1965.

To restrain VC movement further within the delta, the Navy began in early 1966 to augment the VNN forces with its river patrol boats (PBRs). The Mark I PBRs (and their follow-on, the Mark II) were 31-foot fiberglass boats powered and steered by turnable water-jet nozzles and capable of making 29 knots. Their basic armament consisted of two .50-caliber guns, one M-60 machine gun, and a 40-mm grenade launcher.

On 16 May 1966, a VC force with superior fire power ambushed a group of PBRs. This incident revealed the need for quick response. The logical solution was to provide close air support (CAS) for the PBRs. Suitable airfields in the delta, however, were sparse. The only runways capable of handling fixed-wing CAS were at Vung Tau and Binh Thuy. Furthermore, the emphasis on the air war in North Vietnam occupied the large majority of U.S. fixed-wing aircraft.

The VC operated primarily at night. High-speed aircraft have a tough enough time picking out details during daylight hours; target identification at night is extremely difficult. Clouds, rain, or smoke also restricted visibility and necessitated slow airspeeds. Cloud cover meant aircraft either would have to fly below the clouds—in antiaircraft artillery (AAA) range—or come in on top and dive through the clouds, which curtailed target acquisition time. Naturally, the VC took advantage of these conditions.

Unlike their fixed-wing colleagues, helicopter pilots could lay down air-to-surface gunfire 20 meters from a known friendly location. These factors and others like them shifted the burden of CAS for the brown-water Navy away from the fixed-wing community and squarely onto the shoulders of helicopter gunships.

As hostilities escalated, the Army was assigned to support the Navy's inland and coastal operations with these gunships. But this joint arrangement was short-lived, because the Navy sought direct control of air operations to support its river patrols. Thus, the Army withdrew and transferred 8 UH-1B "Huey" aircraft to the Navy in 1966 and extended its allocation to 22 by the end of 1967.

Later in the war, the Navy acquired newer versions of the Huey as they became available, including the UH-1C, UH-1K, UH-1L, and UH-1M. The UH-1C (and later models) with its TH-53-L-11 engine, increased fuel capacity, and improved rotor system permitted the Navy to broaden its helicopter missions. Missions such as the airborne movement of Sea, Air, Land special forces (SEALs) played an important role in

Operation Game Warden. In addition to covert operation, SEAL insertion/extraction teams were used to reconnoiter riverbanks in advance of PBR missions or to provide sniper fire. The UH-11 was unique to the HAL-3 mission because it was an unarmed "slick." This version arrived in time to participate in Operation SEALORDS (Sea, Air, Land, Ocean, River, Delta, Strategy), where its lift capability was useful for carrying SEAL teams. Together with PBR teams, SEAL-laden slicks enabled the brown-water Navy to support the III and IV Corps Tactical Zones' search-and-destroy campaign. The eight slicks built for the Navy transported special warfare personnel on more than 6,000 missions in 1970.

By late 1965 many operational planners recognized that more rigorous actions were needed to tighten the noose around VC fighters. So on 18 December that year, Operation Game Warden was unveiled. Task Force 116 was charged with implementing Game Warden with the intent of "denying the enemy the use of the major rivers of the Delta and the Rung Sat Special Zone." To carry out its mission, TF-116 was assigned 120 PBRs, 20 LCPLs (landing craft, personnel, large), 1 LSD (amphibious transport, dock), 1 LST, and 8 UH-1B helicopters. The Army's 197th Aviation Company provided the Hueys, aircrew, and maintenance support. The first coordinated PBR/Huey mission was conducted on 10 April 1966. To alleviate the complexity of assigning Army helicopters for an extended period in support of naval operations, Navy pilots and crewmen from Helicopter Combat Support Squadron One (HC-1) were brought in to assume the mission. Between June and November 1966, HC-1 established four detachments (numbers 29, 27, 25, and 21) in South Vietnam. The Army crews trained incoming detachment personnel in theater, and then on 30 August relinquished ownership of their UH-1Bs to the Navy. By the end of 1966 the Navy recognized a more specific task structure was needed to expand helicopter gunship operations. Thus, the Navy helicopter community was solicited for volunteers to form a new command dedicated to support riverine action. The Navy began to augment its HC-1 detachments with 80 new volunteers, and on 1 April

1967, Helicopter Attack (Light) Squadron 3 (HA[L]-3 or HAL-3), under the command of Lieutenant Commander Joseph Howard, subsumed all gunship operations from HC-1.

The command-and-control structure consisted of three major task forces. On 1 April 1966 Commander Naval Forces Vietnam was established. Shortly afterward, Coastal Surveillance Force (TF-115) was the first task force to be implemented. River Patrol Force (TF-116) was put in place concurrently with Operation Game Warden and was the organization to which HC-1 (and subsequently HAL-3) helicopters were assigned. As the U.S. commitment increased, riverine tactics continued to evolve in concert with the Army's shift in tactics toward search-and-destroy missions. On 1 September 1966, Mobile Riverine Force, River Assault Flotilla One, was created and arrived in theater in January 1967 under the command of the Riverine Assault Force (TF-117). The officer in command of the helicopter detachment reported operationally to the River Patrol Group commander while reporting administrational to the HAL-3 commanding officer.

HAL-3 evolved eventually into nine detachments that were scattered throughout the Mekong Delta. These were located at five airfields, three LSTs (a fourth LST was rotated off-station for maintenance), and a Mobile Advance Tactical Support Base called Sea Float. A typical detachment consisted of two helicopters, a lieutenant commander as officer in command, with seven additional pilots, eight air crewmen (door gunners), and an assortment of maintenance technicians. According to Howie Price, a HAL-3 pilot, "Airspace operating areas normally were limited to no more than four 'klicks' (1,000 meters) on either side of a main river branch." The HAL-3 detachments prided themselves on their ability to get airborne within three minutes of receiving a call.

The Navy armed its gunships with 2.75-inch folding-fin aerial rockets (FFAR), 7.62-mm flex guns, 40-mm grenade launchers, and lateral-firing cabin-mounted guns. The FFARs were carried in two seven-rocket pods mounted on pylons on either side of the airframe and preferably were fired by the pilot in the right seat. These air-to-surface weapons were outfitted with several different warheads. Rockets equipped with white phosphorous warheads could mark targets, inflict casualties, or start fires. The Flechette round was much loved by pilots but was not used often. The nose-cone of the warhead could be preset to pop off at certain intervals after launch and thus scatter 2,400 one-inch steel projectiles in a variety of patterns and densities. Also available were high-explosive warheads with either impact or proximity fuzes.

One advantage the proximity-fuzed rockets offered over impact-fuzed warheads was that if an impact version hit muddy or swampy terrain, the explosion redirected vertically. High-explosive rockets were preferred over guns in conditions where the aircraft could not get a firing axis that would provide a margin of safety for friendly troops. Oddly enough, in instances of close-contact support, these rockets were more likely to be used than the guns because the ricochets and long ranges of bullets from automatic weapons generated more risk to friendlies than the rapidly decelerating fragments from a rocket. The M151 ten-pound warhead had a lethal radius of around 50 meters. The rocket load-out for a routine fire-team mission consisted of one white phosphorous and six high-explosive rockets in each launcher.

The forward firing guns were mounted above the rocket pods and were commonly called flex guns because they could be fired from the cockpit. Designated the XM-6 weapon system, the twin 7.62-mm, M-60 machine guns were mounted on hydraulic turrets and could be moved through an 80 deg arc (from 10 deg on the opposite side, outward to 70 deg off centerline). The muzzles also could be elevated 10 deg above the horizon or depressed 85 deg downward.

By mid-1970 virtually all the HAL-3 aircraft had had their 7.62-mm flex guns replaced with the M-21 "minigun," a six-barrel Gatling gun capable of firing up to 4,000 7.62-mm rounds per minute.

In place of the twin M-60s, .30-caliber or .50-caliber guns could be used, but the bigger guns required frequent cease-fires to reload. To complete the armament, door gunners manned hand-held (or mounted) M-60s on either side of the fuselage. Occasionally, Mark 18 Honeywell

40-mm grenade launchers or .50-caliber guns were mounted in the cabin door. The grenade launcher could fire tear-gas rounds, which were helpful in flushing out concealed Vietcong. The chief flaws of the .50-caliber machinegun were that it was not as accurate as the smaller guns and it created large volumes of smoke.

With two pilots sitting in a glass bubble on the nose of the aircraft and two door gunners leaning out either side, the detection capabilities of an experienced crew were considerable. What was more, the shape of the aircraft and orientation of the crew enabled at least one member to maintain visual contact, even in a high angle-of-bank turn. Such visual acuity led to another tactical benefit: Navy helicopter gunships invoked the dread of reprisal on the enemy. For all the benefits the AH-1G Cobra two-water brought to the fight, the Vietcong were quick to recognize and exploit its blind and undefended aft end.

Seawolves typically flew in a two-aircraft section called a Light Helicopter Fire Team (LHFT). The lead aircraft was the primary delivery platform, with the wingman providing suppression fire and cover. Dash-2 (the wingman) usually positioned himself in echelon and maintained 500 to 1,000 feet of separation. This wide spacing gave the lead maneuvering room and allotted Dash-2 more time to scan for hostile fire. In addition, Dash-2 flew about 100 feet below the lead for a clear field of fire. The team normally would fly at 1,200 feet above ground level.

Once the target was within a mile of the gunship, the lead aircraft would commence its dive. The LHFT normally would start the profile at 60 knots and accelerate rapidly during the dive, so the pilots had to work efficiently to maintain flight integrity while lining up the target. To make an accurate attack, pilots sought to get as close to the target as possible. On the other hand, to minimize their exposure to hostile fire, the flight needed to maintain airspeed and finish the attack run with sufficient distance and altitude to turn away from the target and pull out of the dive. This was no easy task. By about 800 feet the first rocket salvo was fired, the pilot paused briefly to observe the results, maneuvered the aircraft to refine the firing solution, then fired another salvo. At about 500 feet and less than a klick away, the copilot would commence firing the guns. As soon as the lead finished with his rocket run and began to break away, he provided suppression fire for Dash-2. One technique used at this phase was for the lead to break hard left about 90 and come back 90 deg right. This would put the target at the two to four o'clock position and allow the flex guns and the .50-caliber to deliver flanking fire. Simultaneously, Dash-2 would roll in to deliver the goods from his rocket pods. This maneuver would be repeated as many times as conditions merited or until the firepower was expended.

One difficulty helicopters confronted in Southeast Asia is a condition known as high-density altitude (DA), which conveyed the effect temperature and humidity had on atmospheric conditions. The hot, moist climate diminished engine output and degraded rotor-blade lift. It was routine to have density altitudes that exceeded 3,500 feet at takeoff. Once forward airspeed is acquired, an overloaded aircraft may be able to maintain level flight on a high DA day. But once forward airspeed is depleted—at the end of an attack run or for landing in a confined area, for example—it may not have sufficient power to arrest the rate of descent. Such conditions curbed take-off weight, and more often than not, ship-based aircraft would depart with only ten rockets and less than a full bag of fuel.

Helicopters require less power for takeoff if they can get a running start. Those stationed at airfields could take advantage of this phenomenon and thus carry heavier loads than those on board the anchored LSTs. Rear Admiral Kevin Delaney, formerly of HAL-3, recalls that because of these weight sensitivities, land-based detachments tended to accrue a lot of former football players.

There were, however, two big advantages in stationing helicopters on board LSTs. First the LSTs typically were closer to the action. Second, the aircrews were stationed with PBR crews. This ensured open lines of communication between teams, particularly with regard to premission briefs and post-mission lessons learned. The LSTs had a draft of only 13 feet and thus could move upriver. They also could provide additional firepower with their rapid-firing 40-mm guns, as demonstrated by the USS *Jennings County* (LST-846) in May 1968 when she was credited with 17 Vietcong kills.

HAL-3 was in the thick of things for four years, and 44 Seawolves lost their lives in the line of duty. This small group of naval aviators flew an amazing 78,000 missions. Flight crews averaged 600 combat missions during a 12-month tour. In their first year alone, they fired 155,000 2.75-inch rockets. They had the distinction of flying more combat missions and collectively earned more awards than any other squadron in Vietnam. Among their many awards, the men of HAL-3 received 5 Navy Crosses, 31 Silver Stars, and 156 Purple Hearts.

One example of the dangers that confronted Seawolf aircrews was an incident that occurred on 9 March 1968. Lieutenant Commander Allen Weseleskey was section leader of an LHFT attempting to rescue two wounded U.S. Army advisors. While attempting to land, the two airships were caught by intense ground fire, which wounded a pilot and crewman in the wing aircraft. After instructing his wingman to depart, Weseleskey was joined by an Army AH-1G gunship. In the face of withering fire from automatic weapons, he maneuvered his helicopter into a tight landing zone, picked up the two advisors, and took off. For his extraordinary heroism that day he was awarded the Navy Cross.

Perhaps the greatest benefit Navy attack helicopters provided does not appear directly in any statistic. The hardhitting, dependable reputation that the HAL-3 gunships built lifted Navy morale throughout the delta. Instilled with the knowledge that one of their own was just a radio transmission away, PBR sailors and SEALs were encouraged to push deeper and more boldly into VC territory. HAL-3 was disestablished in March 1972, but the lessons on Navy attack helicopter tactics they left behind undoubtedly will resurface.

Commander Tyler is assigned to Helicopter Combat Support Special Squadron 4, which specializes in naval special warfare support and combat search and rescue in Norfolk, Virginia.

"The Black Ponies"

9

Lieutenant Commander Daniel B. Sheehan, USN (Ret.)

U.S. Naval Institute *Proceedings*
(April 1988): 84–88

IN RETROSPECT, MARCH 1969 was a strange time to base a newly commissioned Navy OV-10 Bronco squadron in South Vietnam. Increasing public pressure to end the war resulted from—and in turn spurred—massive bombing campaigns in and around Vietnam. While Secretary of State Henry Kissinger and the North Vietnamese envoy argued over the shape and size of the peace conference negotiators' table, Jane Fonda and Ramsey Clark marched a little too enthusiastically to their own drummers, and increasingly frustrated U.S. military forces continued to take casualties under an increasingly obvious no-win policy.

But these thoughts were not foremost in my mind when the stretch DC-8 carrying Light Attack Squadron Four (VAL-4) arrived in Saigon. I was a first-tour naval aviator and a plankowner in the only Navy squadron flying OV-10As—the Black Ponies. VAL-4 was the only Navy OV-10 squadron and, as far as I know, the only squadron in Vietnam to use the Bronco in an attack role. Our mission was important: to provide close air support for U.S. and South Vietnamese forces in IV Corps and the southern half of III Corps. Once in-country, we were eager to show what we could do and anxious to measure the impact of our presence upon the heretofore stalled war. In short, we were naive. I certainly was, at least.

As we debarked from our aircraft, we sprouted weapons. Personal pistols appeared from carry-on luggage and Thompson submachine guns emerged from a cruise box with a red cross prominently stenciled on the lid. The unarmed short-timers who casually witnessed this metamorphosis laughed at us. This was lesson number one, in a year full of lessons.

According to the rumor mill, the commanding officer (CO) of VAL-4 had requested naval flight officers (NFOs) to fill the OV-1Os' back seats. All weapon selection and firing were done by the front-seat pilot, and not all flight controls and instruments were duplicated in the rear seat. For example, the back seat had stick and rudder pedals, but no trim controls. The back-seater could lower the landing gear, but not raise them; and he could shut down an engine and feather the prop, but not restart the engine. He could not jettison ordnance or eject the front-seat pilot. The back-seater's primary duties were flight communications and navigation. Occasionally, in routine situations, he took the stick for a few minutes to give the pilot some rest.

Unable or unwilling to assign NFOs, the Navy Bureau of Personnel (BuPers) solicited volunteers from my class of student pilots finishing the advanced multi-engine prop training pipeline. Twelve of us volunteered, but were not told until much later that the squadron considered us back-seaters only. This judgment greatly affected our pre-Vietnam training.

Combined with the twin tasks of forming a new squadron and preparing to move to permanent bases in Vietnam, the stateside training program was hectic: counterinsurgency lectures, OV-10 maintenance training orientation, river patrol boat (PBR) operations familiarization, small arms and hand grenade checkout, and survival school. Survival school was a real eye-opener. Our executive officer (XO) was in one of the first groups of squadron personnel to endure the school's prisoner of war (POW) compound at Warner Springs, California. During his "incarceration," two OV-1Os appeared overhead dropping leaflets.

Ostensibly addressed to the prisoners, these leaflets encouraged them to rally around the XO, who was described as a "Commie killer and street strafer extraordinaire." Naturally the "guards" took notice and gave our beleaguered XO even more unwelcomed attention than before.

Consequently, he insisted that each VAL-4 "POW" group be similarly identified, and often led the leaflet flights himself. Each leaflet batch outdid its predecessor, describing heinous war crimes of unimaginable dimensions in scatalogical terms. This practice continued until the day 200 leaflets hung up on a rocket pod and were held in place by the airstream until the pilot reversed upon landing. The leaflets scattered across Admirals' Row at the North Island Naval Air Station. We were ordered to cease and desist—immediately and irrevocably.

Because of our "back-seater only" status, we nuggets received virtually no flight training in the aircraft. That training was given to the mixed bag of second-tour A-1 Skyraider (Spad) and S-2 Tracker (Stoof) pilots, designated as front-seaters. The omnipresent rumor factory asserted that the jet community spumed fleet seats in a prop aircraft—hence, the assignment of Spad and Stoof pilots from decommissioning squadrons.

One combat-tested Spad pilot was openly contemptuous of a perceived lack of sophistication in the Bronco's weapon system. "The ordnance panel of the OV-10 is simple compared to that of the Spad," he would pontificate. We did not hear that comment again after he launched two rockets into Mexico while attempting to drop flares over a Yuma, Arizona, bombing range.

We rode back-seat on all flights that did not have an instructor there. Back-seaters got in a bit of stick time and even made one or two back-seat landings. When I arrived in Vietnam, I had 20 hours of OV-10 flight time, two of which were in the front seat. This was typical for most nuggets going into combat.

The squadron split into two groups. One operated from Binh Thuy and the other from Vung Tau. Upon arrival in-country, each group set up its own operation. First, the Vung Tau detachment had to depreserve and check-fly our 14 aircraft, which had been cocooned and shipped as deck cargo. The pilot of the first plane to complete a functional check flight let the troops know their efforts were successful, by roaring low over the field and executing a highspeed victory roll. The pilot of the second Bronco imitated the maneuver, but neither his technique nor his airspeed were equal to the task. The nose fell through and the plane disappeared behind a low knoll before it could struggle back to pattern altitude. This same pilot repeated his inept roll on at least one other occasion—a dog-and-pony-show for ranking U.S. and South Vietnamese personnel. After that, he was told to stop, and we named the maneuver after him.

My first fleet-squadron instrument check was in a plane without a tactical air navigation (TACAN) system installed. With the plane's only navigational aid missing, the "up" criterion became the on-time delivery of the sleeping R&R-bound check pilot to Saigon. He woke up at touchdown, signed my papers, and deplaned to catch his freedom bird while I returned to Binh Thuy. That was a far cry from the B-26 check at Corpus Christi.

We began in-country flights to familiarize ourselves with the operating area and to regain aircraft and weapon proficiency. Navigation and communications duties quickly assumed greater importance that they had in the states. All pilots carried all required maps and publications, but we back-seaters bore the brunt of these duties and quickly became adept. All navigation was by visual flight rules, requiring bags that contained 90 charts or more. Standard practice was to use 1:250,000-scale charts for "to/from" navigation. These charts were extensively annotated with province and sector boundaries, and with the numbers of the 1:10,000-scale charts we used for shooting. A standard operating instruction contained the hundreds of callsigns and frequencies of units within our operating area. We back-seaters were very often busier than the proverbial "monkey trying to seduce a football" while navigating to the target area, getting Navy and sector clearance to fire and locating precisely both the target and any nearby friendlies.

Weapon and tactics training was definitely on-the-job; we wrote the close air support tactics doctrine for the OV-10. Because the Air Force and Marine Corps Broncos were primarily used for forward air controller (FAC) and artillery aerial observer (AO) work, they carried only 2.75-inch white phosphorus rockets and—at night—flares. Our Broncos, on the other hand, were loaded with 5- and 2.75-inch rockets, flares, 20-mm. and .30-caliber gun pods, and four internal .30-caliber machine guns. Our ordnance had to consist exclusively of forward firing weapons to keep us from coming under Air Force tactical control. Their cumbersome control system sometimes took hours to grant clearance to fire on targets that needed to be hit immediately.

A standard weapon load for a two-plane section consisted of: eight 5-inch Zuni rockets and either a Mark-IV 20-mm. gun pod or two pods of 2.75-inch rockets for the leader; and eight Zunies and either 14 or 38 2.75-inch rockets for the wingman. Occasionally, an SUU-11 .30-caliber gun pod would be substituted for one of the rocket pods. Later, wing racks were added to each plane, enabling us to carry four additional 5-inch rockets per plane.

The Zuni quickly became the weapon of choice. It was accurate and could be fused for bunkers (base-detonating fuses) or personnel (proximity fuses). At night, it produced a spectacular flame trail; we quickly learned to close one eye when launching.

One senior pilot was notorious for continuing his dive past the pickle point, so he could watch his rockets hit. He would pull off power during the run and break minimum pullout altitude. Not surprisingly, he often holed his own aircraft, by flying through his own shrapnel. When I flew his back seat, I added power for him at 2,000 feet and then initiated pull up at 1,500 feet. These unrequested actions invariably drew a response:

"Goddamn it Dan, don't add power!"

"Yes, sir."

"Goddamn it Dan, don't pull up. I've got it, Dan!"

"Yes, sir."

The next run would be exactly the same.

One night, I was shooting below a 3,000-foot overcast. On pullup, my aircraft passed between the flare and the cloud layer. Rapidly scanning for the leader, I looked forward. For an instant, I knew for certain that I was going to collide with him. And as I tore through my own plane's silhouette on the overcast, I think I used up a year's supply of adrenaline.

U.S. and Vietnamese forces in the Mekong Delta area had not seen much of the supersonic Zuni; they reported a large number of secondary explosions when we used them. Only later did we realize that the troops mistook the rocket's sonic boom for warhead detonation—and then reported the warhead explosion as a secondary.

Listening to friendlies calling in my fire in whispers over the radio because they were too close to "Charlie" to speak normally made me want to whisper back. When your side is that close to the enemy, you've just got to be accurate.

The 2.75-inch rockets were much less accurate and less spectacular than the 5-inchers. It was not uncommon to observe a pair of 2.75-inch rockets—fired together, weaving and rolling around each other before pursuing independent earthward courses. They could be loaded in 7- or 19-shot pods. The 19-shot LAU-3NA pod had two firing settings: single fire, which produced a pair of rockets fired simultaneously, and ripple fire, which launched all 19 rockets in a brief interval. The interval, less than two seconds, was designed to prevent these randomly erratic missiles from hitting each other.

I preferred the ripple setting. With a little more than one G on the plane at the moment of firing, the rockets would spread along the run-in line, which was perfect for treeline targets; with slightly less than one G, they would cluster nicely in a small circular area.

Theoretically, the Mk-IV 20-mm. gun pod was a superior weapon for our type of support. It offered excellent firepower that could easily be used very close to friendly forces. However, it was disappointing in practice. The pod was too heavy for the Bronco's centerline station and designed for faster aircraft. Our 240-knot dives produced insufficient cooling airflow. As a result, overheating limited burst duration and frequency, and caused frequent barrel and jamming problems. On one occasion, the barrels and the nose-assembly's blast-suppressor orifice became misaligned, and the gun shot its own nose off, peppering the underside of the aircraft with shrapnel.

Each flight that fired weapons had to submit a message "spot report" detailing target coordinates, damage assessment, and ordnance expended. The job of drafting this message quickly fell to the back-seater in the number two plane. Tallying rockets was easy enough, but giving an accurate account of the .30-caliber ammunition fired was both tedious and unnecessary. Most of us estimated the totals in round numbers, but I took it one step further. If 1,500 rounds was close, then 1,537 rounds sounded far more accurate and better researched. Plus, some GS-14 would have to add up figures in all four columns.

The flight leader had been impressively accurate, placing his Zunies squarely on target. In deference to his skill, my spot report read "three military structures vaporized." Later, the Commander Naval Forces Vietnam duty officer wanted to know what new weapons we were using. My argument—when you hit a hooch with a Zuni, it is damn well vaporized—was not well received.

I expected our initial operations to concentrate on reacquiring aircraft and weapon proficiency, as well as learning the operating area. But I did not anticipate the public relations campaign we would have to undertake just to find work. Few people outside the squadron had a clear idea of our mission or capabilities. The riverine forces in the field—who theoretically were to be our primary customers—had no inkling of the squadron's presence and purpose, nor did they know how to obtain OV-10 fire support. The operational chain of command did little to ameliorate this situation. They did not develop an employment plan, or even specify combat objectives for the new capability. We were never told, in so many words, to "just fly around and see who wants you." In effect, however, that is exactly what happened. Therefore, as we flew over the rivers and canals, plotting and memorizing checkpoints, we solicited targets from every province and sector headquarters, and every PBR and outpost that had a published radio frequency. Whenever someone listened, we delivered a canned spiel advertising our capabilities—which also listed radio frequencies and telephone numbers for the naval operations center that controlled us.

Gradually, we became known around the Mekong Delta. The squadron operating area was basically between My Tho and the Parrot's Beak for the Vung Tau detachment, and from My Tho to Bac Lieu for the Binh Thuy group. Within these approximate north-south limits, detachment aircraft ranged from the South China Sea westward to the Cambodian border and the Gulf of Thailand. Later in the first year, the Binh Thuy group's area expanded to include Vietnam's southern tip—the Ca Mau Peninsula. There we supported area sweeps and cruise-and-destroy missions by PBRs and Swiftboats based at Sea Float, a nest of barges moored in the middle of the Cua Lon River.

Patrols normally lasted one-and-a-half to two-and-a-half hours. Even if there were no hot targets, we usually shot at something, even if only at abandoned hooches in free-fire zones. Thus, we got some target practice and showed the troops what we could do. Because this aggressive approach got us recognition, we were loath to abandon it.

Operations covering sea-air-land (SEAL) commando, PBR, and Sea Fleet missions required centerline station fuel tanks, which extended our combat endurance to approximately four-and-a-half hours, but reduced our ordnance load. Belly tanks were in short supply, so despite the hazards, we never jettisoned them—even when we took fire.

One pilot ignored low fuel-gauge readings until he was forced to acknowledge independent "fuel caution" and "fuel feed" warning lights. He landed at a South Vietnamese helo field and flamed out from fuel starvation while taxiing to the fuel pits. The remarkable aspect of this story was that he openly briefed us all. He admitted his mistake and taught us all something. That display of honesty took courage and moral fiber.

Each detachment maintained a scramble alert crew ready 24 hours a day in facilities next to the revetments. When alerted, each scramble crew front-seater boarded, started the left engine, and completed as many of the checklists as he could. His back-seater copied coordinates, frequencies, callsigns, and other situational information from the squadron duty officer's list. After the back-seater climbed in, the right engine was started, ordnance armed, and the flight launched. The normal reaction time from alert to airborne was six to eight minutes in daytime and 10–15 minutes at night. Three minutes was our record at Binh Thuy, but we had advance notice and briefed coordinates on the radio.

On night scrambles, we often reacted faster than we could wake up. On several occasions, I fully awoke only after the flight was airborne and had to read a scramble sheet written in my own handwriting to learn where we were headed and what was expected of us. It was an eerie feeling for me to have started an OV-10, taxied, and taken off only minutes before, without any conscious recollection of those events.

As the squadron became more successful, the Navy chain of command, which initially dismissed us to pursue targets on our own, became concerned that the bulk of our firing was done to support Army units, and not the Navy forces the squadron was supposedly chartered to support. This "misuse" of Navy assets was probably politically embarrassing to upper-echelon staff personnel; it was quickly changed. Before, we had flown 80% of our missions during daylight, roaming our operating area at will. Now, almost 90% of our patrolling was done at night along prescribed routes covering the Cambodian border from Ha Tien to Chau Doc, the Vinh Te Canal, and the Parrot's Beak. These "interdiction" missions were supposed to deter infiltration and resupply efforts across the border. In theory, the very sound of OV-10 engines reduced border crossing. In practice, the shift in operations actually degraded squadron effectiveness, but it put the Navy back on politically solid ground. Navy units were again supporting other Navy units.

We shared a good working relationship with an Air Force tactical air support squadron (TASS) flying the infamous Pushme-Pullyou (0–2). They made no attempt to control us. However, they were often able to give us good targets while they waited for their tactical aircraft. This cooperation ended when a TASS FAC told a very tardy flight of F-100s, "Jettison your bombs here. The Navy has already hit my target." From somewhere on high came a directive that Air Force FACs would no longer work Navy air. About a month later, as a TASS FAC tried to steer my flight of OV-10s into a night action involving U.S. advisors in an overrun South Vietnamese Army outpost, an authoritative voice over the radio forbade the FAC's involvement. Ever the professional, he remained on station "inadvertently jettisoning" flares until we could arrive overhead. That such a "my war, my glory" attitude could get in the way of supporting those poor SOBs on the ground was deeply disillusioning. In time, this policy was rescinded.

Within two months of the squadron's arrival in Vietnam, BuPers announced a pilot replacement schedule, which set up an orderly transition from the commissioning crew to fleet replacement pilots over a four-month period. This schedule did not recognize the squadron distinction between front- and back-seaters, and kept junior pilots in-country longer than second-tour pilots. Under this plan and existing squadron policy, the only combat-experienced pilots during the latter part of the transition period would be back seat-limited nuggets. Now we were permitted—even encouraged—to transition to the front seat.

After two front-seat familiarization flights and a solo (with a mechanic in the back seat), I was front seat-qualified. My ordnance training was equally as rigorous. During a one-day standdown from normal patrols, each nugget was allowed one flight on a free-fire zone. My first and last ordnance practice consisted of shooting eight Zunies and 14 2.75-inch rockets at Dong Island. Thereafter, weapon practice was conducted under combat conditions, and pilots now alternated between the front and back seats.

The Bronco was a good weapon platform; I had little difficulty learning to be accurate. The gunsight was not even necessary: the M-60 machine gun tracers indicated where the rest of the ordnance would go. Zunies landed on top of the tracers, while 2.75-inch rockets hit just short of where the tracers hit. For this reason, the transition from back seat to front went more smoothly than the reverse. Front-seaters fumbled with the charts and frequency books and took even longer to master the despised communications/navigation duties than we thought they would. Eventually, our fire teams became even stronger and more professional. My morale certainly improved when I was finally given a chance to fight the aircraft.

Using the Bronco in an attack role in Vietnam was an anomaly. Far slower than jets but faster than helicopters, our planes were initially untouched by hostile (or sometimes friendly) ground fire. The first hits accumulated in aircraft tail sections and slowly worked forward with time.

I was fired on by friendlies one night near Rach Gia. Fifty-caliber tracers (white, not green) passed between my aircraft and the leader's. Not surprisingly, we could not get clearance to return fire to the outpost that clearly was the source of the tracers. I wonder how many times supposedly friendly troops took pot shots at us without our ever knowing it.

The Broncos were lightly armored: fuel tanks were selfsealing up to .30-caliber hits, the center panel of the windshield was bulletproof, and the area directly beneath the crew members' seats was armor-plated. We joked that the rest of the plane was semi-bullet-retardant, at best. It seemed possible to poke a number two lead pencil through the structure just about anywhere on the plane.

The squadron's first casualty occurred when the flight leader was hit in the head by a .30-caliber bullet that penetrated the windshield just to the right of the bulletproof section. The back-seat pilot recovered the aircraft from its 30°, 240-knot dive, pulling out below PBR masthead height, and returned to Binh Thuy. The flight leader, who had helped down an enemy MiG while flying Spads in the north, was dead on arrival.

That was my first exposure to the sudden death we were all subject to, and it was chilling. Intellectually, I knew it could, and probably would, happen. But viscerally, I had naively believed we were just too good, too skilled, too much on the side of the righteous and holy for one of our own to be killed. When it happened, illusions shattered and defenses tumbled. Now I knew that it could happen to me too.

Five squadron mates died that first year in-country. After the first casualty, we lost two aircraft and their crews. These events were upsetting—not only because we lost friends, but also because we never knew for sure just what had happened.

One of the Binh Thuy Broncos, flying number two on a night patrol, took a 10–15° nose-down altitude from 3,000 feet and flew into a 700-foot rock hill, exploding on impact. The flight had been taking sporadic small-arms fire as it transited the area, but had reported no hits. The crewmen of the downed plane made no radio transmissions, nor did either attempt to eject.

The Vung Tau detachment lost a Rung Sat Special Zone patrol—a single OV-10 carrying a Marine Corps air observer. This daily patrol covered the shipping channel into Saigon, flying at 100–200 feet, one-half flaps, and 110–120 knots while the crew searched for signs of ambushes, booby traps, and personnel movements, and called in artillery fire on suspect locations. After failing to return from the patrol, the aircraft, with the crew still on board, was discovered deeply embedded in mud, in an attitude characteristic of a low-altitude stall. Attempts to recover the aircraft failed and nearly resulted in the loss of a CH-47 Chinook helicopter when the lift strap broke, hurling the helo upwards and almost out of control. Too deeply mired for salvage, the wreckage was destroyed.

I do not know if the loss rate in following years was better or worse than in the first. I am certain, however, that the casualty rate and number of aircraft damaged by enemy fire would have been much higher had the squadron been located farther north, in I Corps. The Bronco was just too lightly armored to withstand heavy or high-caliber ground fire, and our tactics would have offered insufficient protection in a much more hostile environment.

I finished my year in Vietnam with 330 missions and a profound sense of relief that it was finally over for me.

My last OV-10 ride was memorable. I rode to Saigon to catch my freedom bird in the cargo section, with two other people. The cargo door had been removed and we were tied in with a cargo strap. Although we had borrowed parachutes, hedging against the bailout possibility, we never gained enough altitude to have used them. At Saigon, I think we had to climb to reach pattern altitude.

Commander Sheehan retired on 1 July 1987 after 20 years of Navy service. From March 1969 to March 1970, he served in VAL-4, as fire team leader, first lieutenant, and quality assurance officer. In subsequent assignments, he flew C-1As, C-130s, C-131s, C-12s, and instructed in T-28s. On a 1975–77 cruise in the *Coral Sea* (CVA-43), he participated in operations supporting the evacuation of Vietnam and Cambodia, and the recovery of the SS *Mayaguez*. He received the Navy Air Medal (23 strike/flight and two individual action awards) and four unit citations, including the Presidential and Navy awards. He was commissioned an ensign through the Harvard University NROTC program in 1967 and was designated a naval aviator in 1968.

10 "Task Force Clearwater: River Security Groups— I Corps Tactical Zone"

Lieutenant Commander Thomas J. Cutler, USN

(Selection from *Brown Water, Black Berets: Coastal and Riverine Warfare in Vietnam*, Naval Institute Press, 1988): 267–82

Northern Frontier

The commander climbed up the wooden rungs of the tower that stood near the northern perimeter of the base. A Marine sentry saluted him as he entered the observation box that sat atop the tower. "Quiet today, sir," the sentry said, and resumed his position gazing out over the sand dunes.

"So far," the commander replied. He picked up a pair of binoculars and looked northward. The day was particularly clear, with a sharp blue sky, and in the distance he could make out the form of a guard tower similar to the one in which he was standing. A spot of motionless khaki just below the roof of the tower told him that a North Vietnamese soldier was probably staring back at him from across the DMZ that separated North from South Vietnam. He knew the distance between the two towers to be just about ten miles.

The commander put down the binoculars and turned to look at the base that had been incongruously inserted into the expanse of sand marking the mouth of the Cua Viet River. The South China Sea sparkled along the base's eastern perimeter, and the jade green of the Annamite Mountains loomed in the distant west. Coils of barbed wire defined the perimeter of the base; sandbagged outcroppings marked its functional structures.

Commander Sayre Swarztrauber had assumed command of Task Force Clearwater the previous fall. It was now the middle of January 1969. He had served in Operation Game Warden for nearly half a year as Commander River Squadron Five before moving to I Corps to become Commander Task Force Clearwater. From his lofty perch, Commander Swarztrauber's attention was drawn to the Cua Viet River below by the sound of diesel engines. An LCU (Landing Craft, Utility) and two LCMs were arriving from Da Nang, ninety miles down the coast. The three craft, laden with food and ammunition, would proceed upriver after a stopover at the Cua Viet base. A PBR and an LCM-6 minesweeper from the Clearwater task force would escort the convoy upstream to Dong Ha, where the cargo would be transferred to trucks for distribution to combat units at Cam Lo, Quang Tri, and various other inland sites. Swarztrauber had made periodic trips up the river himself and had been amazed at how different the Cua Viet was from the Mekong. Just a half mile up the river, the white sand dunes yielded to the shimmering green of overgrown rice paddies. The rusting hulks of armored vehicles and empty, pockmarked huts flanked the river in silent testimony to the earlier clash of armies and the flight of civilians.

Earlier, the PBRs had played a vital role as escorts because ambushes along the river were frequent. Now, with Task Force Clearwater nearly a year old, the minesweepers had become the most important part of the convoys. Ambushes had become infrequent but minings were a constant threat. Since Swarztrauber had taken command, Clearwater personnel were still being killed in action, but none had been lost in firefights along the river. Minings and artillery attacks on the base had been responsible for the deaths. Most of the mines were primitive in construction—often made with such unsophisticated items as inner tubes, clothespins, or toy balloons—but they were deadly nonetheless.

The upstream leg of the trip was the most dangerous because the majority of the mines were free-floating, and moving counter to the current increased the danger of hitting one. It was not uncommon for patrols to open fire on floating hibiscus plants because they closely resembled some of the mines used by the enemy. The downstream leg of the journey was usually accomplished by drifting with the current, which meant that boats and mines would drift along at approximately the same speed, thereby minimizing the changes for contact.

Swarztrauber climbed down from the observation tower and crossed the compound toward the mess hall. He paused for a moment, looking at the base command post, which had been built by placing a standard metal quonset hut in a pit about four feet below ground level, piling sand up around the sides all the way to the roof, and placing multiple layers of sandbags on the roof itself. The building had little in common with the command post in which he had stood watches at the Pentagon during a previous duty assignment.

He entered the mess hall—it too was a semi-buried quonset enshrouded in sand—and headed for the coffeepot. Over the radio in the galley he recognized the voice of Hanoi Hannah, this war's rough equivalent to Tokyo Rose. She was, as usual, predicting the "inevitable defeat of American forces and their Saigon puppets." Some months before, a North Vietnamese artillery round had scored a direct hit on the mess hall, destroying it and killing the solitary cook inside. Shortly afterward, Hannah had broadcast, "You Americans who burrow in the sand like moles, we have destroyed your mess hall. There is no point in building a new one because our gunners will knock it out too." Swarztrauber knew that it had been an empty threat: the NVA gunners were firing their weapons at maximum range and therefore had little or no accuracy. Any hits that occurred were pure luck. By the sheer number of rounds that they expended on the Cua Viet facility, it was inevitable that some would find their mark. The Americans had built a new mess hall despite Hannah's warnings and had named it after the cook who had been killed. The most disconcerting element of the incident was the fact that Hannah knew about the mess hall hit. This meant that the enemy had contacts inside the compound.

As he sipped his coffee, Swarztrauber watched several sailors at the far end of the mess hall eating an early lunch. They sat at the metal tables wearing helmets and flak jackets while they ate. Such was life at Cua Viet. One never knew when incoming rounds would suddenly hit. Since its inception, the Cua Viet base had been subjected to frequent shellings and occasional attempted intrusions by sappers. The prudent man was never very far from his helmet, flak jacket, or personal weapon.

Just after 1700 the shelling resumed. There was a brief hiss followed by a deafening explosion as the first round detonated near the north perimeter. Then, as the warning siren told Cua Viet what it already knew, the rounds fell in random bursts that caused the earth to tremble and sand to rain down in the quonsets. It was both routine and terrifying for the men of Clearwater. All they could do was wait helplessly, praying that the North Vietnamese gunners wouldn't get lucky.

The incoming rounds continued for nearly fifteen minutes. Most of the rounds fell short, dropping into the river or along the north bank, but two hit inside the compound. One detonated harmlessly near the defensive bunkers along the western perimeter; the other struck dangerously close to the ramp, showering sand and light shrapnel over several of the PBRs moored nearby.

At last silence returned, and only hammering hearts could be heard.

Green Wave

In the summer of 1967, the Navy began looking into the feasibility of conducting river patrol operations in the I Corps Tactical Zone, and decided to deploy a section of PBRs there as a test. On 18 September, the USS *Hunterdon County* (LST-838), pregnant with ten PBRs, arrived at the mouth of Cau Hai Bay some seventeen miles northwest of Da Nang. The mission, named Operation Green Wave, was to conduct patrols in the I Corps rivers and lagoons.

Things did not proceed smoothly at the start. Because the LST could not safely enter the bay, the PBRs had to be unloaded from a position offshore. Heavy swells made the process difficult and frequently danger-ous. Once the PBRs got inshore, their lack of familiarity with the area resulted in a number of groundings. Recovering the PBRs after their patrols was equally difficult in the uncooperative surf.

For the first ten days enemy contact was light. Then on the 28th the *Hunterdon County* and her brood moved south to the mouth of the Cua Dai River, approximately eighteen miles south-east of Da Nang. This portion of the operations did not start of well, either. Within three hours of their arrival, four PBRs went to headquarters of Coastal Group 14 for a briefing before their patrol. At the start of their patrol, while still within 1,000 yards of the coastal group base, a heavy barrage of automatic-weapons fire opened up on the four craft. While withdrawing at high speed, PBR-118 received five hits on the starboard side, which perforated the lube oil filters and caused all of the oil to be lost. Both engines seized up and the craft was put out of commission for a while. One VNN junk sailor who had joined them for the patrol was shot through the buttocks and groin in the engagement.

The next day, at a little before noon, PBRs 54 and 79 were operating about five miles up the river near Hoi An when they received twenty rounds of rifle-grenade and about two hundred rounds of automatic-weapons fire. One of the solders was killed when a bullet passed through his flak jacket and struck him behind the left ear; another sailor was wounded. Enemy casualties were unknown.

Three hours later, PBRs 53 and 84, patrolling in the same vicinity, were attacked. Calling in a pair of Army helicopters for support, the PBRs counterattacked and destroyed fifteen huts and bunkers. Again enemy casualties were unknown. Later, however, the same two PBRs and their helicopter support engaged a group of enemy sampans and this time confirmed seven VC killed as well as three sampans sunk and one bunker destroyed. No U.S. casualties resulted on this occasion.

On the 29th, fifteen incidents occurred. Commander Task Unit 116.1.3, the on-scene commander, described the day as a "running gun-battle." The next day, patrols of the area ceased. All of the engagements had involved relatively light enemy weaponry. If the enemy were to bring in heavier armament, which was a distinct possibility, severe losses were almost certain to occur.

On 7 October Operation Green Wave was terminated; the *Hunterdon County* packed up her PBRs and went "home" to the Mekong Delta. A COMNAVFORV report said:

> An immediate analysis of the operation revealed that navigational hazards restricted the PBR speed and maneuverability; intense enemy ground threat precludes proper waterway traffic control by the PBRs; and the grounding and battle damage to 50 percent of the 10-boat task unit precludes sustained operations. Therefore, it was recommended that I Corps PBR deployment be terminated due to unproductive traffic control and heavy enemy weapons and fortifications against which the PBR was not designed to stand.

Perfume and Cua Viet

After the less than spectacular results of Operation Green Wave, it appeared the I Corps had seen the last of the PBRs. But subsequent events were to dictate otherwise.

All U.S. forces in the two northernmost provinces of South Vietnam, Quang Tri and Thua Thien, were supported logistically by the Commander Naval Support Activity, Da Nang. The vast majority of supplies destined for the forces in these two provinces traveled by water from Da Nang up the coast and then inland by river. In Thua Thien Province the supplies were transported up the Perfume River (Huong Giang in Vietnamese—so called because of the fragrance of lotus blossoms that pervades the air there); in Quang Tri it was the Cua Viet River that served as the inland supply route. The enemy did not fail to recognize the military significance of these routes and took advantage of the narrowness of the rivers by planting mines in them and setting up frequent ambushes along their banks.

In response to this threat, General Lewis W. Walt, commanding general of the III Marine Amphibious Force, asked MACV early in 1967 to assign Navy patrol craft to these two rivers to provide protection for the vital logistics traffic. The Navy was reluctant to meet this request because it would mean drawing sorely needed craft away from the Mekong Delta, but they recognized its importance and made plans to accommodate the request. A PBR Mobile Support Base was created by nesting a number of ammi-pontoon barges together and building makeshift repair, berthing, messing, and communications facilities on them. PBR Division 55 was formed and sent north, including the same section of PBRs that had earlier ventured into I Corps during Operation Green Wave.

The units gathered at Tan My on the Perfume and commenced patrols on the river and nearby lagoons on 9 January 1968. Initially, contact was light, but when the Tet Offensive began on 31 January, the PBRs got into the thick of things. A call from personnel at the supply off-loading ramp in Hue said an attack was under way. Eight PBRs charged up the river in response and met heavy rocket, mortar, and small-arms fire when they arrived. They made repeated firing runs on the enemy positions on the north bank of the river opposite the ramp until they suppressed the hostile fire. They held the VC at bay until that evening, when Marines were able to move in and secure the area. The PBRs continued security patrols around Hue for the next several days.

Meanwhile, the overall situation in I Corps had been worsening. As 1967 drew to a close, General Westmoreland had sent his deputy, General Creighton Abrams, to Phu Bai, a military base near Hue, where he could monitor and react to developments more efficiently. When the now-famous siege at Khe Sanh began in the latter part of January, General Abrams reemphasized the need for naval support on the rivers, particularly the Cua Viet. Essential supplies bound for Khe Sanh were traveling up the river to Dong Ha, where they were then airlifted the rest of the way into Khe Sanh. With the eyes of the world focused on this highland outpost, security on the Cua Viet became more important than ever.

In response to General Abrams's request, COMNAVFORV established Task Force Clearwater as a formal command under Captain G.W. Smith on 24 February, incorporating elements already on the scene at Tan My and initiating plans for more units to be sent north for the Cua Viet contingent. Since the VNN base at the mouth of the Cua Viet was frequently under North Vietnamese artillery attack from across the nearly DMZ, and heavy ambushes on the Cua Viet were becoming more and more frequent, COMNAVFORV decided to detach the armored craft of River Assault Division 112 from the Mobile Riverine Force and send them north instead of an additional contingent of the more vulnerable PBRs. The ASPBs from River Assault Division 112 were left behind in the delta, but the ATCs, monitors, and CCB all went and were on station by March.

Commander Task Force Clearwater issued an operation order setting up his organization. He divided the force into two task groups. One, responsible for providing security along the Cua Viet River from its mouth to the supply terminus at Dong Ha, was named the Dong Ha River Security Group. The other, whose area of responsibility was the Perfume River and surrounding waterways as far upriver as the city of Hue, was named the Hue River Security Group. (Unlike other Navy task organizations, Clearwater was never assigned a numerical designation. For its entire existence it remained simply Task Force Clearwater, and its two subordinate task groups retained their unorthodox names as well.) The Dong Ha River Security Group consisted of the ten ATCs, three monitors, and one CCB of River Assault Division 112, while the River Security Group was made up of Mobile Base 1, ten PBRs, and five LCM-6s that had been locally converted into minesweepers.

For administrative purposes the chain of command went from Commander Task Force Clearwater to COMNAVFORV, but operationally Commander Task Force Clearwater reported directly to COMUSMACV (Forward), the post created by General Abrams's move to Phu Bai in late 1967. (In March 1968, COMUSMACV [Forward] changed its name to

Provisional Corps Vietnam and, in the summer of that same year, changed again to XXIV Corps. Commander Task Force Clearwater moved his primary headquarters on 29 February from Tan My to Cua Viet, where it remained until Clearwater was disbanded.) The assembled staff of Clearwater consisted of Navy, Army, and Marine Corps personnel. The force itself was augmented by Army helicopter support, an Army signal (communications) detachment, and Marines from a searchlight battery, assigned to man 24-inch xenon gas infrared searchlights that had been mounted on seven LCPLs subsequently assigned to the Dong Ha River Security Group for surveillance patrols at night.

Once established, the task groups patrolled and escorted convoys. On the Cua Viet, the action was heavy right from the start. A large ambush hit one of the early convoys two miles northeast of Dong Ha, killing the convoy commander, a Navy lieutenant, and wounding four other Navy men. A few days later, an ATC hit a sizable mine that flipped the 66-ton craft upside down, causing extensive damage, severely wounding one crew member, and killing six others. And so it went for the Dong Ha River Security Group convoys. Rocket, mortar, and artillery attacks against the base at Cua Viet and against Dong Ha were also frequent.

Once the fury of the Tet Offensive had subsided, the presence of large numbers of American forces in the area kept the situation on the Perfume River quiet for a while. Occasional attacks on the river and at the ramp in Hue kept the river security group from ever letting down their guard, however. By June the area around Hue and along the Perfume River proper was largely pacified, so Commander Task Force Clearwater obtained permission from his Army boss to expand the mission of his forces into a wider and more diversified patrol effort similar to the Game Warden mission in the delta.

The Hue River Security Group forces began to conduct a variety of operations in the waterways and lagoons that connected with the Perfume River, including troop insertion and coordinated operations with elements of the Army's 101st Airborne Division, cordon and search scenarios, medical and dental aid visits to the villages and psychological operations. In line with the latter category, an astute intelligence officer recognized that the people of Hue consider the dragon to be powerful and honorable, so the psychological operations material passed out in the area carried a dragon symbol, and the PBRs flew dragon's-head flags. Consequently, the people began referring to the PBRs as *Tau Rong*, or Dragon Boats. This, combined with the aid missions and the fact that the Communist forces, while in temporary control of Hue during the Tet Offensive, had massacred at least three thousand of its citizens, yielded positive results. The local people were primarily receptive to the American patrols and often willingly cooperated. Even on the Cua Viet farther north, the local people seemed hospitable to the American forces. On many occasions, children along the banks hailed the patrolling craft and turned over caches of weapons and ammunition they had discovered near their villages.

Continued attacks on the Cua Viet led to the reevaluation of Clearwater's response capability. The analysts decided that the speed of PBRs was more important in responding to attacks than was the armor of the Mobile Riverine Force craft in protecting the boats from damage. Consequently, they requested more PBRs. Ten PBRs taken from the Rung Sat Special Zone arrived to join the Dong Ha River Security Group, five in May and five in June. With the arrival of these additional craft, most of the River Assault Division 112 craft were detached to return to operations in the delta. Six ATCs temporarily remained with the group to serve as minesweepers until five LCM-6s could be locally transfigured for the minesweeping role.

Also in June, an earlier request for more assets for Clearwater was answered by the arrival of the Navy's three PACVs. Having proven themselves to be of little real value in Game Warden and Market Time because of their limitation on narrow waterways or in the open sea, and having had the most success in the open environment of the Plain of Reeds during Operation Monster, the PACVs had the potential to fare well in the lagoons of the Hue River Security Group's operational area. Indeed, the strange craft worked well as part of Clearwater. The environment of lagoons, rice paddies, and salt flats in the Hue area was ideal for the PACVs. They worked exceptionally well in conjunction with ground forces, able to pursue fleeing enemy troops no matter what combination of land-water escape route they tried. They also performed well for medical evacuation and emergency troop extraction. The Navy's PACVs continued to function as part of Clearwater until mid-1969, when they were slated for retirement. So well had they performed that the Army replaced them with air-cushion vehicles of their own.

As time went on, the efforts of Clearwater, coupled with sweeps by the Army and Marine ground forces in the region, virtually eliminated the ambush threat from the banks of either river. But enemy mining continued, so minesweeping assets in addition to the LCM-6s were incorporated in Clearwater, including MSMs, an LCM-6 conversion that had previously served in the Rung Sat as part of Mine Division 113, and MSBs. In late 1969, two of the MSMs were outfitted with a mine-hunting sonar, called Shadowgraph, that was capable of locating mines in the rivers.

Task Force Clearwater remained in service for several years, fighting to keep the vital I Corps rivers open. The enemy continued to mine, and Clearwater forces continued to sweep, patrol, and escort. Then in June 1970, in a relieving ceremony, the Vietnamese Navy assumed the mission of Clearwater and the Americans were reassigned in Vietnam or went home.

In a 1971 article, Commander R.L. Schreadley wrote a fitting tribute to the men who served in Clearwater:

> During the long months of the northeast monsoon the climate is probably the country's worst, with cold, grey and rainy days following each other in seemingly endless succession. Outside the river mouth(s), there are restless shoals and a pounding surf. Some of the unsung heroes of this war are the captains who guided low-powered and frequently age-weakened ships and craft through the treacherous white water of the . . . hazardous channels in northern I Corps. . . .

The men at Cua Viet lived little better than moles in heavily bunkered huts burrowed down among the sand dunes. When the rain stopped falling, the sand, fine-grained and gritty, began to blow, accumulating in drifts before the huts, sifting through screens and under doors, finding its way into lockers and between sheets and even into the food the men ate.

In October 1968, a program was initiated to gradually rotate all Cua Viet personnel back to Da Nang or Tan My, to ensure that no one would be required to spend more than six months at the advanced base. It is a tribute to the splendid morale of our sailors, and their sense of sharing in what was in many ways a unique drama, that many volunteered to stay on and finish their tours at Cua Viet.

Postscripts

The mission of Task Force Clearwater never did go away. American forces continued the patrols, sweeps, troop insertions and withdrawals, and escort duties until June 1970, when they turned the assets and the mission over to the VNN. Throughout their tenure, the American sailors, Marines, and soldiers carried out their unheralded task in the face of sudden death or maiming by the lurking mines, frequent artillery barrages, and ever-present sapper units. Their existence as an operational unit is rarely acknowledged in the Vietnam War literature, but their mission was an important one and their conduct under fire was above reproach. The names of those who died are carved in black granite, yet they, like so many whose deeds or passing do not catch the myopic eye of their countrymen, are relegated to the obscurity of collective sacrifice.

Commander Swarztrauber went on to command the *USS Decatur* (DDG-31) and ultimately retired from the Navy as a rear admiral. He received his Ph.D. in international studies from American University, has written extensively, and is currently the superintendent of the Maine Maritime Academy.

11 "The Mobile Riverine Force, Vietnam"

Commander Dan Dagle, USNR

U.S. Naval Institute *Proceedings*
(January 1969): 126–28

THE BUILDUP OF U.S. FORCES in Vietnam's Mekong Delta has brought a concept of operations into being which is entirely new to the 20th century U.S. military man.

While making contingency plans for sustained operations in the Delta, planners were faced with designing a force that could operate in a 26,000-square-mile, poorly drained area interlaced with one of the densest networks of inter-connecting rivers, streams, and man-made canals in the world. The major problem confronting them was mobility. There was, at that time, nothing in Army, Navy, or Marine Corps inventories that could be counted upon to move and support the required number of troops to and from an operational area in this environment.

Drawing upon U.S. experiences in amphibious warfare and from information gained from examining the tactics and equipment used by the French Dinassauts and their protégé, the Vietnamese River Assault Groups which are the only military forces having had recent experience in conducting riverine warfare, the planners developed a concept which was derived from, but not directly related to either of these approaches. The new concept has now materialized as the Mobile Riverine Force.

The Mobile Riverine Force (MRF) is a marriage between separate Army and Navy commands that are tasked with conducting search and destroy operations in areas dominated by waterways. The Second Brigade of the Army's Ninth Infantry Division provides two battalions to conduct the actual search and destroy operations, while boats especially designed to support them are under the command of the Commander, River Assault Flotilla One, operating as Commander, Riverine Assault Force (CTF 117). These boats lend the necessary transportation for the troops between their base and the area of operation. After disembarking the troops, the boats take up blocking positions to keep the enemy from using the neighboring waterways as a means of escape or for bringing in reinforcements. From these positions, the boats are also able to provide gunfire support for the Army. The troops and the assault boats normally stay in the area of operations from two to four days before returning to base, where the troops dry out and rest, and the boat crews resupply their boats, and conduct preventative maintenance.

There are five types of boats assigned to the two squadrons, River Assault Squadrons 9 and 11, in the flotilla. The primary boat is the armored troop carrier (ATC), which is designed to carry a 40-man, combat-loaded infantry platoon. The command and communications boat (CCB) has the communications equipment necessary for the squadron or boat division commander to control the boats and to provide the Army with a forward command post. The Monitor carries the heaviest weapons and is the "battleship" of this armada of boats. The assault support patrol boat (ASPB) is the Monitor's destroyer, which has a shallower draft and higher speed than the other boats. It provides the operation with a primary mine sweeping and quick reaction capability. And lastly, the refueler is basically configured as an ATC and carries helicopter fuel in bladders installed in the well deck.

Some of the ATCs and refuelers have been modified by adding a helicopter landing platform over the forward deck for use by HU-l-D

(Huey) and OH-23-G helicopters. This innovation considerably expands the force's capability for command and control, troop lift, resupply, and medical evacuation. Several ATCs carrying helicopter decks have been fitted with enough medical equipment, including refrigeration units for whole blood, to support medical clearance units. These boats are moved into an area where the wounded can be taken aboard and treated while, at the same time, the boat retreats to an area secure enough to bring in evacuation helicopters.

With the exception of the 50-foot ASPBs, built specifically for River Assault Flotilla One, all the boats are modified LCM(6)s. These boats are well armored and, again, with the exception of the ASPBs, their armament includes bar armor, installed 18 to 20 inches outboard of the armor plate. This serves to detonate recoilless rifle or rocket rounds so that their full force is dissipated over a larger area of the armor plate, or, in the case of shaped charges, so that their heat column is deformed.

The boats carry a considerable amount of firepower to the area of operations. The ATCs, CCBs, Monitors, and refuelers all have the same gun turret arrangement aft, with one belt-fed, .50-caliber machine gun mounted in both the port and starboard turrets located just aft of the conning station. These guns have MK-18 grenade launchers mounted on top of their receivers. Just behind the two .50-caliber turrets is a third turret on the centerline that houses a belt-fed, 20-mm. cannon. Each of these boats carries 7.62-mm. machine guns, and hand-held weapons. In addition to the weapons common to all four of the LCM(6) conversions, the Monitors and the CCBs carry a forward turret in which is installed a 40-mm. cannon and a .50-caliber machine gun; the Monitors have an 81-mm. mortar installed in a pit between the forward mount and the conning station.

The ASPBs pack a 20-mm. cannon, an 81-mm. mortar, a twin .50-caliber or 7.62-mm. machine gun, and two MK-18 grenade launchers.

These boats and the troops they support are in turn supported by a Mobile Riverine Base (MRB), capable of moving anywhere on the many major waterways in the Delta. The base, which is commanded by the Commander, River Support Squadron Seven, a second hat for Commander, River Assault Flotilla One, consists primarily of two self-propelled barracks ships, the *Benewah* (APB-35) and the *Colleton* (APB-36), one barracks barge (APL-26), one boat repair ship, the *Askari* (ARL-30), a support LST that serves as a supply warehouse, and two tugs (YTB). Another LST ferries supplies from the supply depot to the base. From the base, the boats and the embarked Army units move into the surrounding territory to conduct their operations. At random intervals, the base is moved to a new location, sometimes back to old ones to allow the embarked battalions to cover a much larger area of the Delta than would he possible working from a fixed base. In addition to providing the Army and Navy people with a place that has dry bunks, hot food, showers, air conditioning, laundry, and some recreational facilities, the base's mission includes maintenance and repair of the boats and logistic support for the embarked units.

As might be expected, this union of Army and Navy forces has not been without problems but, considering the fact that neither service had any previous experience in riverine assault warfare, they have been relatively few in number. Most have been solved by co-operative ingenuity. As a result, the Mobile Riverine Force—with its specially trained men, its uniquely designed ships and boats, and its unique intra-service spirit— has repeatedly proven its effectiveness in battle.

Commander Dagle formerly served on the staff of Commander, River Assault Flotilla One, Vietnam.

12

Comment and Discussion on "The Riverine Force in Action"
(W. C. Wells, Naval Review 1969, pp. 46–83)

Commander C. L. Horowitz, USN

U.S. Naval Institute *Proceedings*
(November 1969): 116–18

PERHAPS ONE DAY some intrepid soul or souls will wade through the after-action reports, operations orders, and eye-witness interviews, and write a definitive history of the Mobile Riverine Force (MRF), perhaps now, in view of its apparent reduction of scope in Vietnam.

My own relationship with the MRF began on 3 October 1966, when I reported at ComPhibTraPac, Coronado, California, a prospective Commanding Officer of River Assault Squadron Nine (RASNine). The various elements of River Assault Flotilla One, including the Flotilla staff, Squadrons Nine and Eleven staffs, and the squadrons' boat crews, gathered for the counter-insurgency, survival, and Vietnamese language training at Coronado, and then boat, operations, and weapon training at the Naval Inshore Operating Training Center at Vallejo, California. RASNine was officially commissioned on 3 November 1966, the first of its kind in the U.S. Navy since the Civil War. I took command on 16 December 1966, when my squadron staff and River Assault Division 91 (RivDiv 91) completed training and reported to ComRivFlot One for duty. On 4 January 1967, my staff, RivDiv 91, and an element of the RivFlot One staff departed for Vietnam.

We arrived at Tan San Nhut airport at 0200 on 7 January, and later that day embarked in the USS *Whitfield County* (LST-1169) our mother ship, in which I broke my pennant. An advance contingent of the Riv-Flot One staff, in-country since October 1966, provided our liaison with ComNavForV and USMACV. They provided us with three converted LCM-6s, borrowed from the Vietnamese Navy, and we outfitted these with boat kits provided by the flotilla staff. We then proceeded with the LST and the three boats to Vung Tau. We worked feverishly for a week, double and triple crewing our three boats to enable the crews to get as much boat handling and firing training as possible before the first of the Army's Ninth Infantry Division arrived for operational training, which began on 18 January. As the boat crews became more adept at beaching and retracting, providing covering fire, and boat handling and night navigation in the swamps of the Rung Sat Special Zone, so, too, did the Ninth Division troops learn how to move in mud like quicksand. The *Whitfield County* progressed in troop handling from over-the-side wet nets to using alongside Ammi pontoons for mooring boats and staging troops.

Gradually, the number of boats borrowed from the Vietnamese Navy grew, to even armored troop carriers (ATCs), one monitor, and one ancient command and communications (CCB) boat, complete with bullet holes in the windshield. Eventually, radar was placed in the CCB, which greatly simplified pre-dawn transits from Vung Tau to the Rung Sat Special Zone.

In mid-February, Viet Cong (VC) units were attacking shipping on the Long Tau river, the main shipping channel from the South China Sea to Saigon. My boats, and Third Battalion, 47th Infantry Battalion, were co-located at a base camp on the Long Tau, about midway to Saigon. We engaged in ambush insertions and extractions; in night-time interdiction patrols; in using boats to guard the flanks of troop perimeters; in waterborne employment of 81-mm. mortars when the ground was too soft; and in command control of boat operations from a helicopter. Since only two-thirds of the troops were in the field at one time, with the other third drying out on board the LST, we had a regular round trip shuttle added to our other duties. Our combined efforts were successful in preventing further attacks on shipping, and we also salvaged some useful intelligence documents from sampans beached by river patrol boat (PBR) interdiction patrol.

In late February, the remainder of the RivFlot One staff, RivDiv 92, and part of RAS Eleven arrived in Vietnam. The USS *Henrico* (APA-45) arrived to relieve the *Whitfield County* as mother ship and to provide the necessary extra berthing and staff spaces required. Once again the boats were double-and-triple-crewed to provide operational training for the newly arrived crews. In March, the first three of our newly converted ATCs arrived in-country, and were a welcome addition to our tired and overworked Vietnamese boats.

By 10 April, RAS Nine had turned over all the Vietnamese boats to RAS Eleven except the monitor, and I took RAS Nine to Dong Tam for employment in the Delta, while RAS Eleven took over duties in the Rung Sat Special Zone, operating from the USS *Montrose* (APA-212) in Vung Tau Harbor. In Dong Tam we lived on board the APL-26 and the YRBM-17 provided our maintenance support. Both were moored in Dong Tam Basin.

On 15 May, a combined force of RAS Nine and RAS Eleven boats supported two infantry and one artillery battalion on an assault on the Cam Son area, the first major action of the MRF in the Delta. We suffered our first sizeable personnel and material casualties, but all hands performed admirably. For the first time, battalion medical aid teams were embarked on selected ATCs, and they proved invaluable in the early treatment of the wounded. A repair boat was also employed in the operating area to repair battle damage sufficiently to allow the damaged boats to transit to Dong Tam.

The first week in June, the entire Mobile Riverine Force anchored in the Mytho River off Dong Tam. Apart from the APL-26 and YRBM-17, which remained in Dong Tam basin, the force consisted of the USS *Benewah* (APB-35), the force flagship; the USS *Colleton* (APB-36); the USS *Askari* (ARL-30); and the USS *Vernon County* (LST-1161), temporarily attached. Embarked were two infantry battalions, the Second Brigade staff, River Assault Squadrons Nine and Eleven, and the RivFlot One/RivSupRon Seven staff.

On 18 June, the MRF was anchored in the Soi Rap River, preparatory to the first operation in Long An Province, and a day later began the second major battle of the MRF. On 21 June that battle ended, with a cost to the VC of over 200 dead by body count, thereby rendering ineffective the VC presence in Long An Province for a year. It also demonstrated the effectiveness of the organic weapons of the boats against an enemy in ambush positions. RivDiv 92 saved an ambushed infantry company from annihilation, and my CCB's 40-mm. gun knocked out a VC .50-caliber machine gun position by having its fire spotted by a battalion commander circling overhead in his helicopter. This same .50-caliber had previously knocked out two UH-1B choppers and one a medevac helo. ComRivRon Eleven arrived on the scene with a monitor and resupply of 40-mm. ammunition, and proceeded up a shallow stream to knock out another .50-caliber position with his monitor's 40-mm. gun. Of course, artillery, air strikes, and helicopter gun ships contributed the major share of the body count, but the boats had kept the VC entrapped until they could be hit by the heavy stuff. The embarked battalion aid teams once again proved their worth; I was one of their patients during this battle.

The MRF continued campaigning throughout the Delta, from Ben Tre to Sa Dec, projecting itself into former VC sanctuaries, and dishing it out ten-to-one in kill ratio. Innovations such as a flight deck attached to an ATC to make it a floating helo pad, ATCs equipped with a flame-throwing Armored Personnel Carrier, and the arrival of the Assault Support patrol boat (ASPB) added to the MRF's effectiveness. The ASPB boat crews, who arrived in-country well before their boats, received good operational training by filling in for wounded members of other boat crews. As a matter of fact, I don't know how we could have kept all our boats operational without this pool of available personnel. We also had joint operations with the Seventh Division, Army of the Republic of Vietnam (ARNV) and temporarily incorporated the Fifth Vietnamese Marine Battalion into the MRF. The Marines' leadership and performance were outstanding.

I was relieved on 29 December, arrived in Saigon on New Year's eve for processing, and arrived at McGuire Air Force Base on 3 January 1968, completing to a day my year's odyssey in Vietnam. The success of the Mobile Riverine Force, conceived, trained, and committed to combat in a relatively short time, is a tribute to the officers who led it and to the combat sailors who manned it.

"SEA LORDS"

13

Commander Richard L. Schreadley, USN

U.S. Naval Institute *Proceedings*
(August 1970): 22–31

IN THE FALL OF 1968, more than 38,000 officers and men had been assigned to U.S. Naval Forces Vietnam. The three principal task forces— TF-115 (Market Time), TF-116 (Game Warden), and TF-117 (Mobile Riverine Force)—were either at or rapidly approaching their full programmed strength.

By almost all measurable criteria the task forces had achieved a high degree of effectiveness. There had been no known attempts to infiltrate large shipments of men or arms into South Vietnam by sea since the Tet offensive earlier in the year. Possibly, small intra-coastal transshipments may still have occurred, but if they did, it was at a high cost to the enemy because of the intensive and well co-ordinated Market Time air and sea patrols. These patrols had forced the enemy to reorient his entire logistics system and to organize and construct networks of infiltration routes in the Demilitarized Zone, in Laos, and in Cambodia. Porters and communications-liaison personnel, consequently, were no longer positioned in sufficient numbers along the coast to handle large quantities of material arriving from the sea.

Game Warden units patrolled the major rivers and enforced curfews and regulations established by the government of Vietnam. In the month of September 1968 alone, 111,628 boardings and inspections of river craft were recorded by the river patrol force. In the nearly roadless Delta, control of the rivers means control of a large segment of the population, for boats are relied upon almost exclusively in the rural areas to get from one village to another and for the movement of goods and crops to market. Moreover, fish from the rivers and seas are important in the Vietnamese diet, and wet-rice farming, the principal agricultural activity, requires an intricate system of irrigation dikes and canals.

The Mobile Riverine Force—the U.S. Navy's "great green fleet of the Delta" combined with elements of the U.S. Army's 9th Infantry Division—compiled impressive records of enemy troops, weapons, and structures destroyed. Hard-hitting and wide-ranging, the MRF was credited by General William Westmoreland with having "saved the Delta" during the dark hours of the 1968 Tet offensive.

Despite these very real accomplishments by the several task forces, however, the enemy still controlled large areas of the Delta and still infiltrated and circulated large numbers of troops and large quantities of war materials into South Vietnam via the waterways of the Delta.

We had known for a long time that enemy supplies for the III and IV Corps areas of Vietnam crossed the border from Cambodia. With blockade in the traditional sense held not to be within approved national policy, the task of interdicting Communist logistic movements from Cambodia was complicated.

As early as January 1964, the essential futility of a sea barrier to infiltration without an attendant border interdiction effort was acknowledged when a team of eight naval officers headed by Captain Phillip H. Bucklew met in Saigon to study the problem. Recommendations were made at that time to develop a border patrol force equipped with high-speed small craft. In succeeding years, the men, boats, bases, and aircraft required to mount such an effort were acquired and readied. Beginning in late October 1968, a plan called SEA LORDS (Southeast Asia Lake, Ocean, River, and Delta Strategy) became the catalyst which welded those assets into a combined force to thrust, at long last, seapower inland athwart enemy infiltration routes between the Gulf of Thailand and an area northeast of the Cambodian "Parrot's Beak."

The old idea of largely independent operations by the three task forces was changed to create what really amounted to a brown water task fleet in which the light and fast PBRs and PCFs ("Swifts") assumed the roles of destroyers and cruisers in support of the heavily armored and slow riverine assault craft which could be likened, in our analogy, to battleships and troop-carrying amphibious ships.

The fractured nature of the ground command structure in IV Corps, where most of the troops were Vietnamese, posed special problems. Though in theory centrally controlled, in practice, division commanders, province chiefs, and even district chiefs exercised a surprising degree of autonomy in the employment of the forces assigned to them. The limits of geographic areas of responsibility were rigidly observed and as these areas were often divided one from the other by major rivers, the rivers themselves, of primary concern to the Navy, were often a "no man's land" insofar as the ground forces were concerned. The success of SEA LORDS hinged on the co-operation and mutual support of sea, ground, and air forces. If it was desirable to combine the best features of the three naval task forces for the proposed operation, it was essential that adequate ground and air assets be committed to ensure the initial and long-term success of the new strategy.

On 20 October 1968, ComNavForV made his initial SEA LORDS proposals to the Senior Advisor IV corps Tactical Zone (SA IV CTZ), a U.S. Army Major General, calling them naval support for the 1968–1969 IV Corps Dry Season Campaign. The broad objectives to be sought were: the interdiction of Viet Cong infiltration routes from the Gulf of Thailand to the upper Mekong River; the control of vital trans-Delta inland waterways; and the penetration of rivers in the enemy-held Ca Mau Peninsula by Market Time raiders to "stir up the enemy and keep him off-balance." Market Time, Game Warden, and Mobile Riverine Force operations would continue at nearly the established levels, with assets loaned by the task force commanders to the "First Sea Lord," the overall commander for SEA LORDS operations, on an *ad hoc* basis. These assets could be made available through a lessening of Market Time PCF patrols, which would permit the Swift boats to assume new responsibilities in the lower rivers and to undertake the raider incursions. The PBRs relieved on the lower rivers could then be employed on the proposed barriers. The heavy MRF craft were already under-employed, owing to a chronic shortage of ground forces to support riverine operations.

A study of the map showed that the most desirable water route to exploit for interdiction of Communist logistics entering IV Corps from Cambodia was the Rach Giang Thanh-Vinh Te Canal route linking Ha Tien on the Gulf of Thailand with Chau Doc on the upper Mekong River. This route, however, closely parallels the border and the expected heavy risk of real or contrived border incidents dictated against the positioning of a SEA LORDS barrier there until the concept was tested and proved in a less sensitive area. It was decided, therefore, that two parallel canals some 35 and 40 miles removed from the border to the southeast— the Rach Gia di Long Xuyen and the Cai San—would be used to form a double barrier and inaugurate the SEA LORDS interdiction campaign. "Interdiction in depth" had its attractiveness from an operations analysis point of view, and, at the same time, two waterways would be opened for friendly traffic. In conjunction with this barrier, river patrols would be strengthened from Long Xuyen through the Yam Nao Crossover to the Mekong.

The second objective of SEA LORDS—control of vital trans-Delta inland waterways—would be accomplished by the removal of obstructions to navigation in the Cho Gao Canal linking the Yam Co and My Tho Rivers, by strike operations along the Mang Thit-Nicolai Canal which joins the Co Chien and Bassac Rivers, and by reopening of the Bassac-Bac Lieu Rice Route in the lower Delta. Penetration of rivers in the Ca Mau Peninsula, the third objective, actually began before the formal proposals to SA IV CTZ. A Swift boat incursion of the Cua Lon River on 18 October 1968 is usually considered the first of the SEA LORDS operations, though a few earlier such operations by Market Time PCFs are recorded.

The Senior Advisor IV CTZ endorsed the Navy's proposals, and organization for SEA LORDS proceeded rapidly. Captain (now Rear Admiral) R. S. Salzer, U.S. Navy, then Commander of the naval component of the Mobile Riverine Force, was designated First Sea Lord and assigned a staff of nine officers and six enlisted men at SA IV CTZ headquarters in Can Tho. ComNavForV was given the task force designator 194. First Sea Lord became CTG 194.0 and exercised operational control of these three additional task groups: TG 194.5, Coastal Raiding and Blocking Group; TG 194.6, Riverine Raiding and Blocking Group; and TG 194.7, Riverine Strike Group. First Sea Lord was directed to designate one of the three task force commanders to command each specific SEA LORDS operation, with CTF-115 normally expected to command SEA LORDS incursions from seaward, CTF-116 riverine and blocking operations, and CTF-117 riverine strike operations involving large commitments of ground forces. On 25 October, CTFs 115, 116, and 117 were directed to report to First Sea Lord for operations.

On 2 November, the first of the barrier campaigns, later given the name "Search Turn," was initiated by an assault on enemy positions along the Rach Gia di Long Xuyen Canal. Heavy MRF craft and supporting ground troops succeeded in securing the waterway in a five-day operation which resulted in 21 enemy killed and the capture of sizeable quantities of arms and ammunition. On completion of the assault phase, a permanent naval patrol was established with primary emphasis given to the western ends of the barrier and the network of perpendicular canals running north from Rach Gia to Ha Tien. This was the general area through which, according to our intelligence reports, the principal Communist commo-liaison lines passed.

While this operation was in progress, other SEA LORDS forces were employed in clearing the Cho Gao Canal and, by 6 November, that waterway was open to navigation. Later in the month the Tan Dinh and Dung Island complexes in the Bassac River were sealed off by a naval blockade while ground forces conducted sweep operations. Market Time raider operations moved into high gear as areas in the Ca Mau which had long been considered exclusively the domain of the Viet Cong were repeatedly penetrated by daring Swift boat patrols.

The second of the interdiction barriers was established on 16 November 1968 as a direct result of a young Swift boat officer's initiative. The desirability of a barrier along the Rach Giang Thanh-Vinh Te waterway at the Cambodian border, and the reason for rejecting that location for the first SEA LORDS interdiction effort, have already been mentioned. On 14 October 1968, however, as the SEA LORDS proposals were being put into final shape, Lieutenant (j.g.) Michael Bernique, U.S. Naval Reserve, took his PCF into Ha Tien on the Gulf of Thailand for an "R&R"—a brief respite from the rigors of his Market Time patrol. While there, he was told that a Viet Cong "tax station" had been established a few miles up the Rach Giang Thanh. Acting on his own authority, he immediately proceeded up the river which, because of the political sensitivity of the Cambodian border, had heretofore been off-limits to Navy patrol boats. Upon rounding a bend in the river, he suddenly encountered the "tax collector" and seven armed men near the river bank. So surprised were they that they failed to open fire on the American boat until it had closed to a range of less than 100 yards. By then it was much too late, and in a brief exchange, three of the enemy were killed and the rest fled. A few moments later, while the crew of the Swift boat was busy collecting documents and discarded enemy weapons, small arms fire was taken from the river bank and promptly returned. Agent reports later indicated that two more of the enemy were killed and two wounded in the second exchange.

When his audacious acting became known, Bernique faced one of two possible consequences—a severe reprimand for taking his PCF into a prohibited area, or an award for conspicuous valor in routing the Communist extortionists. He was summarily ordered to report to Saigon and personally explain his action to ComNavForV who, upon hearing Bernique's colorful account of the foray up the Rach Giang Thanh, chose to award him the Silver Star. The Rach Giang Thanh was henceforth known as "Bernique's Creek."

The incident heightened the Admiral's interest in a border barrier and after discussions with ComUSMACV, plans were made for a follow-up to the 14 October incursion which would test the ability of naval forces to transit the whole of Bernique's Creek and the Vinh Te Canal.

Early on the morning of 16 November, therefore, three PCFs supported by two Seawolf helicopters entered the Rach Giang Thanh from Ha Tien with orders to proceed via the Vinh Te Canal to Chau Doc. On the way they were to interdict enemy supply lines, kill or capture Viet Cong tax collectors, board and search suspicious craft, gather intelligence, and conduct psychological operations. The officer-in-charge of the lead PCF was the redoubtable Bernique and once more he became involved in an incident which was to bring him face to face with the Admiral.

Shortly after the PCFs departed Ha Tien they acquired intelligence, later confirmed, which gave the location of two Viet Cong "tax stations" on the river ahead. Armed men were sighted at the first indicated location and a brief firefight ensued. Twenty minutes later, further up the river, a similar group was detected and taken under fire. The Swift boats then continued their journey without further incident. Within a few hours of these engagements, however, ComNavForV was advised by the Naval Intelligence Liaison Officer at Ha Tien that the District Chief there had information that the armed men who had been engaged by the PCFs were not Viet Cong, but Cambodian para-military bandits, the Khmer Kampuchea Kron (KKK). Ten were said to have been killed and another four wounded. Furthermore, ten "South Vietnamese women of Cambodian origin" were reportedly slain in a large sampan shot up by the PCFs.

The incident resulted in a protest by Cambodia to the International Control Commission and for a time threatened the continuation of naval operations on the waterway. ComNavForV immediately dispatched Captain Roy F. Hoffman, U.S. Navy, to make a thorough on-scene investigation. Good fortune again smiled on Bernique. The Commander of the Ha Tien KKK battalion was located and stated flatly that the armed men involved in the shootings were Viet Cong and not KKK. An examination of the sampan where the alleged killing of the ten women had occurred failed to reveal bloodstains or other evidence of the carnage that supposedly took place there. Finally, still and motion pictures taken at the time of the firefights supported the PCFs' version of what had happened and indicated that their fire was well controlled and directed.

In retrospect, it appears quite possible, if not probable, that the charges made against the PCFs were part of a Communist plot to discredit the naval effort along the viral Cambodian border and to force its suspension by political means. Strong pressures in that direction were experienced, but ComNavForV and ComUSMACV recognized that to abandon the patrols in the face of such ill-founded charges would be interpreted by the people who lived along the border as a sign of weakness and would rend to degrade further Saigon's tenuous hold on the area. Furthermore, it was believed that resolve on our part to prevent infiltration at the border on a waterway entirely under South Vietnamese jurisdiction might encourage Cambodia to increase the security of its own border from illicit Communist crossing. Patrols were continued, with PCFs assigned to the western end of the barrier or Bernique's Creek, and PBRs backed by river assault craft on the eastern end. Falling water levels, steep banks, and inadequate ground support were serious obstacles to overcome in the following months, but except for a brief period in late January and early February 1969, a naval presence was maintained. The operation, at first called "Foul Deck" and later, as the Vietnamese Navy assumed a growing share of the effort, "Tran Hung Dao," became the second most active of the interdiction barriers.

A third barrier operation was launched on 6 December 1968. Given the code name "Giant Slingshot," this campaign achieved by far the most dramatic and telling effects on enemy infiltration of all the interdiction barriers.

A scant 30 miles west of Saigon a peculiarly drawn border thrusts the Cambodian "Parrot's Beak" deep into Vietnam's III Corps area. The Parrot's Beak had long been notorious as the source of Communist logistic movement across the border and well documented infiltration routes had been traced which entered South Vietnam between the Vam Co Tay and Vam Co Dong Rivers and then turned either south to the Delta or east to supply the Viet Cong in the countryside surrounding the capital. These two rivers flow on either side of the Parrot's Beak on converging courses to the southeast and to a confluence roughly 15 miles south of Saigon. There they form the Vam Co River which continues in the same general direction to a second confluence with the Soirap River and thence the flow continues to the South China Sea.

The waterways described above formed what appeared to be a slingshot into which the Parrot's Beak neatly fit. The nickname Giant Slingshot followed naturally.

Once again ground support had to be sought, but this time the job proved easier. Most of the troops in the Giant Slingshot area were U.S. Army, and Rear Admiral W. H. House, who had assumed the post of First Sea Lord upon Captain Salzer's detachment, called on Commanding General II Field Force Vietnam (CG II FFV) and got his endorsement of the operation.

Because of the distances involved and the inability to position support ships on the rivers above the low bridges at Tan An and Ben Luc, an entirely new basing and support concept had to be devised for Giant Slingshot. The Advance Tactical Support Base (ATSB) was designed and constructed to meet that requirement. Built on 30 feet by 90 feet "ammi" pontoon barges which can be rowed with relative ease virtually anywhere on the rivers, the typical ATSB consists of three or more ammi barges on which are constructed berthing and messing facilities, storerooms, a tactical operations center (TOC), water purification equipment, generators and other assorted machinery. Ammunition is usually stowed in a bunker ashore. Each ATSB is provided with a nearby helo pad. Food, ammunition, and fuel are carried to the advance bases by shuttle boats which make regular runs from primary staging sites further down the rivers. The river craft supported by the ATSB moor outboard the ammi barges during periods when they are not employed.

Living conditions are austere and life is hard for the sailors at an ATSB. There is practically never any liberty, and recreation facilities are all but nonexistent. In spite of this, however, morale has in general remained high, due in no small measure to the inspired leadership of the young lieutenants and senior petty officers who have shouldered such heavy responsibilities at these remote outposts.

ATSBs were established at Tuyen Nhon and Moe Hoa on the Vam Co Tay and at Tra Cu and Hiep Hoa on the Vam Co Dong. The site at Hiep Hoa was later abandoned in favor of one at Go Dau Ha and, coincident with Operation Double Shift in July 1969, an additional ATSB was placed at Ben Keo near the important city of Tay Ninh. The USS *Askari* (ARL-30) and the YRBM-18 were positioned at Tan An, pending the arrival of Mobile Base II, a sophisticated four-ammi complex specially constructed in the United States with the latest in afloat habitability features and extensive boat repair capabilities. The USS *Harnett County* (LST-821) provided support at Ben Luc for the patrol boats until the completion of a shore support base there.

The story of the *Harnett County* at Ben Luc is well worth recording. The river at Ben Luc is little more than 200 meters wide, and the surrounding countryside, despite its nearness to Saigon, was far from secure at the time of the ship's arrival to support Giant Slingshot operations. Furthermore, it was known that the Viet Cong had made a standing offer of $100,000 for the destruction of a U.S. ship.

The *Harnett County* arrived at Ben Luc early on the morning of 12 December 1968, escorted by 19 PBRs. The absence of any meaningful bank security dictated that the ship return each night to a "safe" anchorage near French Fort at the confluence of the rivers. This routine was followed every day until 27 December, when the ship arrived at Ben Luc to stay. The threat from enemy mining and sapper attack was constant. Twice the ship was struck by enemy rocket fire. In spite of "living under the gun," the performance of the *Harnett County's* crew of 10 officers and 135 enlisted men was magnificent and contributed in no small way to the great success of Giant Slingshot. A measure of the increased output demanded and delivered can be seen in four statistics. Message traffic increased by more than 400%. Commissary issues more than doubled, requiring the ship's galley to remain open from 0600 to 0100 daily. Special security watches continuously employed 10% of the crew. And, finally, river bank clearance operations in the vicinity of the ship's anchorage (called by the crew "Operation Chop Chop") employed an average of 55 men, 10 hours a day, for 30 days.

Also piled on top of routine ship's work were the repair and support of the operating PBRs, the greatly increased frequency of helicopter operations from the LST's deck, and the endless struggle with piping and cooling systems fouled by the river mud and silt.

From its very inception, Giant Slingshot was characterized by frequent, heavy clashes between our patrol boats and enemy forces intent on maintaining the lines of communication to their Cambodian storehouse. Extremely large quantities of arms, munitions, and supplies were uncovered in caches buried along the river banks, proving beyond any doubt that vital enemy infiltration lines were being interdicted.

The fourth and last of the Delta interdiction barriers was established on 2 January 1969 when naval patrols began operations on the La Grange-Ong Lon Canal from Tuyen Nhon on the Vam Co Tay to An Long on the Mekong. Called "Barrier Reef," this operation joined Giant Slingshot in the east with the two-tiered barriers in the west, Search Turn and Tran Hung Dao. The northern ring of interdiction was then complete. The enemy would no longer be permitted to move his men and supplies with impunity from Cambodia into III and IV Corps areas. A naval "tariff" had been imposed on those shipments, measurable in terms of men and supplies captured or destroyed, but incalculable in respect to what was deterred from ever being sent. As of 8 December 1969, the tangible results of the four interdiction barriers were evident.

Because our boat crews are not able to leave their boats to search for enemy dead, the reported numbers are undoubtedly low. A better indication of interdiction activity, therefore, is the number of firefights experienced.

With the barriers in place, the mobility of boats could be used to excellent advantage in reacting to shifting enemy pressures and probes. With relatively little disruption to existing organization and logistics, naval assets could be relocated rapidly from one area of operations to another. Nowhere was this capability better demonstrated than in Operation "Double Shift" in July 1969, when 105 U.S. Navy and Vietnamese Navy boats were quickly concentrated in the Vam Co Dong River, north of Go Dau Ha in response to serious enemy threats to the city of Tay Ninh. This sudden and impressive display of naval power, brilliantly orchestrated by the on-scene commander, Lieutenant Commander T. K. Anderson, U.S. Navy, was credited by Commanding General II FFV with having prevented the enemy attack on Tay Ninh from the southwest.

On two separate occasions the mobility of the boats was increased spectacularly when giant Army Skycrane helicopters were used to lift some of them into new areas of operations. In May 1969, six PBRs were skyhooked to the upper Saigon River, and in June six more were lifted to the supposedly inaccessible Cai Cai Canal. Both operations achieved tactical surprise.

In the Ca Mau Peninsula the success of the PCF raider incursions pointed to an increasing naval role in long-term efforts to pacify the area and return it to the Saigon government's control. Lessons learned in the development of the ATSBs for Giant Slingshot, and a shortage of the ground forces necessary to protect a base established ashore, speeded the design and deployment of a Mobile Advance Tactical Support Base (MATSB), which was located for easy defense in the middle of the Cua Lon River near the abandoned and ruined city of old Nam Can. The MATSB was constructed on nine ammi pontoons and provided a base for PCFs and river assault craft. Communist "tax collectors" were routed and a concentrated psychological program was launched to encourage the resettlement and economic development of the Nam Can area. Called "Sea Float," this combined U.S. Navy and Vietnamese Navy operation was begun in June 1969 and was an almost immediate success. Thousands of visitors flocked to the Navy complex. Commercial woodcutting and fishing revived. Within a few months of Sea Float's establishment more than 9,000 people had resettled in its vicinity. The success of the venture led, in late September 1969, to the positioning of a somewhat smaller MATSB further north in the Ca Mau peninsula on the Ong Doc River. This operation was given the code name "Breezy Cove."

Though not interdiction barriers in the sense of the Cambodian border operations and the continuing Market Time sea patrols, Sea Float, Breezy Cove, and other naval operations in the Delta complemented and strengthened the interdiction strategy of SEA LORDS. As the barriers drastically curtailed the enemy's ability to infiltrate supplies to his forces in the Delta, those forces were progressively weakened and neutralized. By denying the enemy sources of revenue and support in the Delta itself, the process was significantly speeded. Finally, by encouraging economic development and peaceful commerce in areas freed from the scourge of Viet Cong extortion, the ultimate goal of the naval war in the Delta— meaningful pacification and renewed confidence in and support of the Government in Saigon—became clearly attainable.

As each operation progressed, concerted efforts were made to integrate units of the growing Vietnamese Navy. The military desirability and political necessity to "Vietnamize" the naval war were evident long in advance of SEA LORDS planning. It seemed obvious that the Vietnamese

Navy's hopes to relieve the U.S. Navy of its operational responsibilities in the war as soon as possible would be considerably enhanced if the SEA LORDS objectives were met. ComNavForV's view was that the surest and quickest way to achieve both the SEA LORDS objectives and the turnover of operational responsibilities was for both navies to work together.

A remarkable organization was put together on the rivers and canals of the Delta. SEA LORDS meant unity of command and rapid response to changing tactical situations. Relatively junior officers and men were often placed in positions of extraordinary responsibility. Tactics and techniques were developed and tested in the heat of combat, and at times even borrowed from the enemy, improved upon, and used to defeat him. An illustration of the latter is the waterborne guardpost, a refinement of the favorite enemy tactic of ambush. Using silent boats, night observation devices, endless patience, and a large measure of sheer guts, our Brown Water sailors turned the tables on the enemy. Frequently the would-be ambusher became the ambushed.

The high practitioner of the waterborne guardpost in Vietnam was a Chief Signalman named Bob Allen Monzingo. During his stint on the river as a patrol officer with River Division 593, Monzingo was awarded three Bronze and two Silver Stars. One of his more memorable engagements with the enemy occurred on the upper Saigon River in the summer of 1969. He set his two-boat guardpost at dusk in the midst of a driving rainstorm, at a spot where the river runs shallow and relatively narrow. His men had just gotten into their ponchos and rain gear and were steeling themselves for a long, wet and uncomfortable night, when word came from the cover boat as follows: "Chief, I see a *bunch* of them out there."

Monzingo had to look several times to believe what he was seeing on the near bank, only a few dozen yards away in the gray gloom. Columns of enemy soldiers were filing past, heads lowered because of the driving rain, shoulders bent by the weight of heavy weapons, rocket launchers, and packs. He quickly estimated that there were at least 80 and perhaps a full company of the enemy. It seemed incredible that they were still unaware of the presence of the PBRs.

Without hesitation he gave the necessary orders. The engines on both boats leaped to life and they backed rapidly into the middle of the stream, pouring deadly fire into the surprised ranks of the enemy. The boats themselves were soon taken under fire from both banks and it was obvious that Monzingo's guard post had been set right in the middle of a planned, large-scale crossing attempt by the Communist soldiers. Helicopter gunships, tactical air, and artillery were called in to support the PBRs. Other boats from further down river rushed additional firepower and ammunition to the scene. It was more than two hours before the last of the enemy guns were silenced.

The next morning when ground troops swept the area 41 enemy soldiers were discovered where they had fallen. Eight more were pulled from the river or off the banks by the patrol boats.

Monzingo's engagement on the upper Saigon River illustrates the high degree of co-ordination achieved between air, ground, and afloat units. Never more than minutes away, the Navy's UH-1B Seawolf helicopter and its OV-10 fixed wing "Black Pony" aircraft are the river sailor's best friends in a firefight. Artillery support from Army fire bases and from howitzers on Navy monitors is almost always available and accurate. Electronic sensor teams warn of enemy movement and increase the detection probabilities of the barriers.

In all these ways, SEA LORDS put a new face on the naval war in Vietnam. Imaginative and inspiring leadership provided the plan and lighted the fires. A dedicated and fearless collection of sailors, soldiers, and airmen made the plan work and kept the fires burning.

Commander Schreadley enlisted in the Navy in 1949 and served at sea in the USS *Forrest Royal* (DP-872) and USS *Leyte* (CV-32). A graduate of Dickinson College in 1955, he was commissioned an ensign in the Naval Reserve that same year. He has been gunnery officer in the USS *Hank* (DD-702), an Instructor of Naval Science at the New York State Maritime College, Mine Warfare Officer on the Staff of Commander Mine Squadron Four, Officer in Charge of USS *Greenwood* (DE-679), and Commanding Officer USS *Sturdy* (MSO-494). From 1967 to 1969, he was a postgraduate student at the Fletcher School of Law and Diplomacy where he received his M.A. degree in 1968 and his M.A.L.D. degree in 1969. He is now assigned as a Special Assistant on the Staff of Commander Naval Forces Vietnam.

"Swift Raiders"

14

Commander Richard L. Schreadley, USN

U.S. Naval Institute *Proceedings*
(June 1984): 53–56

THE SOUTH CHINA SEA teems with fish. One particular variety, a silver flat fish with a tail deeply notched like the fletched end of an arrow, is a powerful jumper. When frightened by the sound of an approaching boat or larger fish, it darts off in a long series of arching leaps that carry it perhaps six or eight feet clear of the water. Sailors on our Swift boat patrols occasionally tried to shoot this fish out of the air with a shotgun. But they rarely succeeded.

When the weather was good, the 80-odd mile trip at sea from Cat Lo to the mouth of the Bassac River was enjoyable. When a sailor had been ashore for awhile, breathing the pungent and varied odors of Vietnam and choking on the exhaust fumes of cyclos and Hondas, clean sea air and salt spray were like letters from home.

The officer in charge on this Swift boat run to Coastal Group 36 on the Bassac was a lieutenant (junior grade). Five enlisted men were his crew. There was a quartermaster second, a gunner's mate third, an engineman third, a seaman, and a Vietnamese trainee fresh from the Saigon boat school. The year was 1969.

The lieutenant was a firm believer in the Vietnamization program. "The sooner we train them to do our job, the sooner we go home." He took a personal interest in his Vietnamese trainee and had him on the wheel driving as soon as the boat cleared the harbor at Vung Tau. When he got so that he could steer a decent compass course, he was taught how to light off and read the Fathometer and the Decca radar. He seemed to learn fast, in spite of the language difficulty, and because he was so busy, he forgot to get seasick.

When the trainee had absorbed about as much as he could in the pilothouse in one sitting, the gunner's mate took him in tow and began checking him out on the after machine guns. There, he had some trouble. He was a small, frail man, scarcely more than a boy, and it was difficult for him to jack the heavy machine gun. But with much struggling, his face knitted in grim determination, he managed it.

Coastal Group 36 had the reputation of being the best outfit in the Vietnamese Junk Force. You could almost tell that just by looking at it. Its junks were out where they belonged: on the river checking traffic. Its base, on the right bank of the Bassac opposite Dung Island, was well maintained. Weeds were chopped down and grass trimmed; the concertina wire was in good shape; and garbage was not piled in or near the compound. Buildings were reasonably well roofed and screened. Most impressive was the absence at midafternoon of bored and underemployed "junkies" who were quite noticeable at poorly managed bases.

Coastal Group 36's senior adviser, a wiry U.S. Navy lieutenant, had nothing but good to say about the two counterparts he had trained during his tour there. Both had been competent, honest, and willing to take advice. "How lucky can you get?" he asked. How lucky indeed. The lieutenant had pioneered effective but dangerous skimmer boat operations during his tour at the Coastal Group and never suffered a scratch. A few months later, his relief would die in his first week on the job while on a skimmer operation.

There were three Swift boats assigned at this time to a rotating patrol on the lower Bassac, and all three rendezvoused at Coastal Group 36 at the adviser's request. The in-chopping boat from Cat Lo was the last to arrive.

The adviser's hootch was spacious, airy, and clean. An enlisted adviser was brushing a fresh coat of paint, river patrol boat green, on the outside of the hootch. On the inside, a bamboo bar occupied one entire wall. The shelves in back of the bar were lined, not with bottles, but with rows of shaving cream, toothpaste, tropical candy, razors, writing paper, and more. It looked like a ship's store.

"I get a new sundry pack every couple of weeks," the lieutenant explained. "I'm afraid to ask them to cut down on their shipments because then, you know, they'd probably knock them off altogether. A couple of years ago, a guy here was reduced to bumming used toothbrushes off the boats. Now we can return the favor. You see any used toothbrushes there you like, go on and help yourself." He got everyone a cold beer, and we gathered around a table in front of the bar.

Decentralization of both planning and execution was a valuable feature of Delta operations. This permitted quick response to enemy initiatives and local developments. It had not always been thus. At certain times in the past, it had taken weeks to clear a locally planned operation, but under SEA LORDS (Southeast Asia Lake, Ocean, River and Delta Strategy), it could be handled in a few hours.

The adviser had hard intelligence that a new VietCong bunker complex had been thrown up on the banks of a narrow canal running off the Bassac, about 20 miles to the north. The canal was believed navigable by Swift boats, and he could arrange with Binh Thuy to provide Black Ponies (OV-10 Bronco aircraft). The plan was to rendezvous off the canal entrance at daybreak the next morning, saturate the area with mortar fire, and then, with Black Ponies overhead, the three Swift boats would slip into the canal, locate the bunkers, and destroy them. Vegetation on both sides of the canal was known to be dense. Harassing and interdiction fire would be directed at the banks as the Swift boats made their entrance. Coastal Group 36 junks would provide a blocking force on the river in case the Swifts flushed any Viet Cong.

The officers of the Swift boats studied the chart of the area. The senior among them designated which boats would fire mortars and where and established the order of the boats. His would lead. The chart showed that there were numerous bends in the canal.

"Stay close and watch your gunners. Let's not shoot up each other," the senior officer cautioned. Then, the planning conference was over.

They were a colorful lot, the Swift boat skippers. One sported a handlebar mustache and closely cropped hair. Another wore a rakish Australian jungle hat. Yet, they still had the air of competent professionals. They had been made to shoulder heavy responsibilities at an early age, and they earned their burdens well. The officer with the Australian hat waved it over his head and let out a cowboy yell as his boat gunned away from the Coastal Group base. The mustachioed officer merely grinned and called out, "See you tomorrow."

The Swift boat that had arrived from Cat Lo spent the night patrolling the waters northeast of Dung Island. She ran darkened and at quiet engine speeds, and the only craft she sighted throughout the night was the Coast Guard boat assigned to patrol the adjacent coastal area on the few occasions that she probed the mouth of the river. Since the boat remained under way on the broad Bassac, the mosquito problem was nearly avoided and half the crew at a time could catch some sleep. On his watch, the Vietnamese trainee learned to navigate by radar. The Decca's scope painted a beautiful picture.

Sometimes, a faint light flickered on the banks, probably coming from a fisherman's hootch, and occasionally a few illumination rounds lit the northern horizon near Can Tho. But the boat spent most of the night wrapped in darkness on a black river under a jeweled sky. Finally, in the early hours before dawn, the boat left her patrol area and headed north to rendezvous with the other two Swift boats.

The first mortar rounds crashed ashore shortly before 0600. The Swifts stood well off the entrance to the targeted canal and bombarded the area for almost 20 minutes. Crews were suited up in flak jackets and battle helmets and two Black Ponies were overhead when the lead boat entered the canal, followed at about 100-yard intervals by the other two.

The canal was much narrower than it appeared on the chart. Tree limbs reached out and brushed both sides of the boats in the worst areas, and the forward gunners frequently had to duck to avoid overhanging foliage. All three boats laced the banks with bursts of machine gun fire as the column snaked slowly down the waterway. About a mile into the canal, the men spied a few ruined and abandoned hootches on the north bank and several rotting sampans. Farther on, the boats passed the abutments of a fallen foot bridge, which had once spanned the canal. Something, perhaps a piece of the old bridge, bumped the keel of the first boat.

Trailing vines, brilliant wild flowers, unfamiliar trees, and heavy green foliage gave the area the appearance of forest primeval. Were it not for the clatter of the machine guns, the canal might have passed for a nature trail in the Florida Everglades.

The first bunker was sighted a little beyond a junction with a smaller cross canal. Beyond the junction were others, set back about ten or 15 yards from the bank and apparently newly dug. They were well screened from the air, and the Black Ponies probably could not see them.

With the slamming of their own machine guns, it was difficult to tell when and how the boats were first hit. Probably, one or more claymores (antipersonnel mines) hidden in the trees were command fired from one of the bunkers. The second boat in the column, followed almost immediately by the first, reported a wounded man on board. A 180° turn was ordered, and as the boats cleared the area, they marked it with smoke grenades. The Black Ponies immediately attacked the area and within a few minutes reported four secondary explosions.

The Swift boats cleared the canal at high speed, their wakes pounding and washing over the banks. Within 100 yards of the Bassac, a large geyser of water, observed by the Black Ponies, sprouted between the first two boats. Almost certainly, someone well back on the bank, trying to guess by engine noise alone the correct moment to fire, set off a command-detonated mine. It caused no damage, and a moment later the three boats broke into the bright early morning sunlight on the Bassac.

The two wounded men were not seriously hurt. An after gunner had taken shrapnel in the calf of his right leg. An ensign, a prospective officer-in-charge on his first indoctrination patrol, had a small piece of shrapnel imbedded above his left eyebrow. A helicopter "dust-off" was not considered necessary, and the boats carried their wounded to Binh Thuy, another 15 miles north on the river.

As they went about securing weapons and squaring their boats away, the sailors on the Swifts seemed as calm and unruffled as if they had just finished a leisurely breakfast. On one boat, the skinny Vietnamese crewman—he had earned the title—had to be reminded to remove his heavy flak jacket, and his too-large helmet was more than a little askew. But he had survived his baptism by fire, and he would make it.

The Bassac River sprang to life. Sampans plied the river, and children appeared on the banks. Incredibly, the whole affair had consumed less than an hour.

"River Power"

15

Commander Thomas R. M. Emery, USN

U.S. Naval Institute *Proceedings*
(August 1970): 117–21

TAKE A COMBINATION OF 28 river patrol craft, a U.S. Navy landing ship, tank (LST) with two UH-1B Seawolf helo gun-ships embarked, two Vietnamese Navy (VNN) ships, 400 Vietnamese ground troops, 350 U.S. sailors, and a floating headquarters/support base in the middle of a river deep in Viet Cong (VC) territory, and you have one of the most unusual operational arrangements in the annals of naval history. Add to this riverine potpourri the requirement to develop a village and build a shore base on a hostile river bank in the jungle, and the ingredients for Operation Seafloat are all present.

This unusual "mix" of naval units was inherited by a U.S. Navy commander who was given the job of moving his "force" up the Cua Lon River in the southwestern portion of the lower Ca Mau Peninsula.

The mission was a simple but important one—establish a U.S. and Vietnamese presence in an area which had belonged to the Viet Cong since the Tet offensive of 1968, and was one of several traditional VC sanctuaries in the Delta. With the presence established and secured, the balance of the task was to: deny the VC freedom of movement throughout the lower Ca Mau Peninsula; provide a base for the military and economic pacification effort in an area rich with natural resources; develop a site for future use by the Vietnamese Navy as a riverine operations base; and finally, to serve as a haven, during the turbulent monsoon season, for U.S. and Vietnamese Navy small craft, thereby eliminating the need for them to return to established bases at An Thoi or Cat Lo.

This operation—Seafloat—conceived by the Commander Naval Forces, Vietnam, became a reality in June 1969, and is fulfilling its charter, and more.

From a tenuous beginning, the operation has become a catalyst for the development of the lower Ca Mau Peninsula and the entré for the return of the government of South Vietnam (GVN). Nha Be, a river city just south of Saigon and the location of Naval Support Activity (NSA), Saigon, was where the pieces later to become Seafloat were assembled.

Nine ammi pontoons (floating containers), each 30 by 90 feet, were joined together and compartmentalized, providing housing facilities for 150 men. Seafloat also had the capability to feed and support 700 U.S. and Vietnamese Navymen. The support facilities included all those normally associated with conventional shipboard life—diesel generators for power, fresh water and diesel fuel storage, an ammi which provided landing space for three helicopters, berthing, a mess hall and galley, two large reefers, an operations center, communication facilities, and a sick bay. The pontoons were given the nickname "Turtle Ammis," because of their overhead mortar protection.

All the ammis, with most of the support personnel embarked, were loaded into three landing ships, dock (LSD), for the transit south. Two days after leaving Nha Be, the mini-convoy arrived at the mouth of Bo De River. The LSDs deposited their cargo, and the ammis were then towed up the Bo De and into the Cua Lon river by tugs. Harbor Clearance Unit (HCU) One completed the mooring, and Seafloat was home, off the bank of what was once Nam Can City. That site was selected because, militarily, it provided access to both the Gulf of Thailand and the South China Sea, since the Cua Lon was navigable in both directions. Ships and craft moving from Saigon in the north to the Gulf of Thailand could, therefore, avoid the longer voyage around the southern tip of the peninsula.

Historically, the site provided psychological significance, since it is adjacent to Old Nam Can City. Nam Can was a flourishing city of some 4,000 people prior to the 1968 Tet offensive. The Viet Cong forced the residents to abandon the city, using a tight blockade. Faced by starvation and the threat of annihilation, the Nam Can residents moved north into more secure areas. Subsequent battles between Allied and enemy forces destroyed Nam Can City. Seafloat's presence gave notice to the VC that the deed of ownership was about to be changed.

The manning concept of Seafloat was a joint venture right from the start. This writer was commander of Seafloat, and designated Commander, Task Group 115.7. The deputy commander was Vietnamese. There were some American sailors serving in the psychological warfare and intelligence capacities, but the VNN provided most of the men for these jobs. U.S. Navymen handled all the support functions—cooks, watchstanders, boatswain's mates, gunner's mates, radiomen, and hospital corpsmen. Both American and Vietnamese Navymen and equipment were used to handle the tactical operations—the force needed to put "muscle" into Seafloat.

Initially, this "muscle" was made up of a Vietnamese Navy landing ship, medium (LSM), which was fitted with dental and hospital vans; a VNN landing ship, infantry, large (LSIL); a U.S. Navy patrol vessel, gunboat (PG); an LST, eight patrol craft, inshore (PCF), and a detachment of two Seawolf helicopters. The Seafloat commander also had at his disposal a platoon of SEALs, underwater demolition teams (UDT), explosive ordnance disposal (EOD) detachments, and ten Kit Carson scouts (former VC who had rallied to the GVN cause).

This mixed bag of assets was immediately employed to keep the VC off-balance by the vigorous patrolling of the rivers and canals, by conducting SEAL operations within and without the Seafloat area of operations (AO), and, in conjunction with Vietnamese regional forces obtained from the district capitol, by conducting troop sweeps throughout the AO.

Once the anchors had been secured by HCU-1, the immediate problem facing Seafloat was how to handle its own defense. With no ground troops yet available, the problem was intensified. In reviewing the possible methods open to the enemy for attack, this author had the following firepower to counter any such attempt: four 81-mm. mortars; six .50-caliber machine guns; ten M-60 machine guns; and numerous small arms. In addition, there were three .50-caliber machine guns, two M-60s; and a 3-inch, .50-caliber on board the LSM, LSIL, and PG. The Seafloat commander could also call upon the combined firepower of the Seawolf helos, OV-10 Broncos, and "Swift" boats.

The enemy had four possible attack options: direct assault by ground troops, mining or sapper attacks, attack by sampans, or mortar attacks.

The first type of attack was not likely, because Seafloat was in the middle of the river, and tactical air strikes were available. The second type of attack was less than likely, because of a variable six-to-eight-knot current, anti-swimmer nets, sentries, and night observation devices. The third kind of attack was possible, but not likely, because of the surface craft available to counterattack. The fourth was the most likely attack, but discouraging to the enemy because of the harassing and interdiction (H and I) fire, troop sweeps, interdiction posts, and sensors.

The most effective deterrent to an attack in Seafloat's bag of tricks was the tactic of "randomized pressure." This strategy used the various ground, afloat, and air assets of Seafloat in varying amounts, at different times, and at different places—to keep the VC off balance. It was so effective that the Seafloat environment was soon secure enough for a new village to bloom near the ruins of Old Nam Can City. And, as the village grew, so did an effective psychological operations (PsyOps) program.

The basic concept of the PsyOps program was contact with the local people to tell them of the GVN aims; how they could enhance their economic condition and well being by breaking away from the VC. These goals were attained by: conducting tape and live broadcasts from PCFs and the Seawolves; providing medical and dental assistance from the

Vietnamese LSM; giving lectures to groups of Vietnamese which came on board Seafloat units; and by continuing with the successful tactical operations which were already showing gratifying results.

It was difficult to measure the effectiveness of PsyOps, but "bench marks" soon began to appear: women told PsyOps personnel of the location of grenades; men in sampans related to crews of the PCFs of an impending ambush, and many Vietnamese turned in pieces of ordnance. As the local populace realized that Seafloat was there to stay, a dramatic change occurred—a village emerged. There, in the southern tip of Vietnam, a naval task group had sired a village. About five miles east of Seafloat, on the north bank of the Song Cua Long, small groups of woodcutters and fishermen began building their thatched huts. Some merchants from distant cities put up ax-sharpening shops, sampan motor repair shops, and small food and beverage stores were opened. The date was 1 August 1969—a month and a half after Seafloat arrived.

Five months later, the population had grown to 4,000. On 15 December 1969, the province chief officially designated the village as Tran Hung Dau I (Tran Hung Dau was a famous Vietnamese naval hero). He named a hamlet chief and assigned a province redevelopment cadre to assist with the initial political and economic structuring of the village. On 8 March 1970, in the schoolhouse at Trang Hung Dau I, a ceremony was held to recognize the academic achievements of the top students in the two separate classes. This ceremony marked the emergence of the village as a community—a community that had begun with a handful of woodcutters listening to a U.S. Navy PCF loudspeaker carrying a message from the Vietnamese Navy. In six months, a GVN-controlled village was carved out of VC country. Seafloat was properly doing its job.

The tactical operations, meanwhile, that had permitted this PsyOps program to flourish, were producing similar successes. The area proved so lucrative that a company of the Mobile Strike Forces (MSF), under the command of the 5th Special Forces, on three different occasions, had been employed for a month in the Seafloat AO. With the arrival of these troops, seven river assault craft were added, including armored troop carriers (ATC), assault support patrol boats (ASPB), a 105-mm. howitzer monitor, and a "Zippo" flame-thrower monitor. The PCFs were augmented by two VNN PCFs and ten VNN yabuta junks, mounting .50-caliber machine guns, and a 60-mm. mortar. More ground troops were added by the Vietnamese—80 Biet Hai (VN sailors who had received extensive infantry training), a platoon of regional forces, and more Kit Carson scouts.

The statistics (after eight months) were impressive—408 VC killed in action (KIA), with a kill ratio of enemy to friendly of 27-to-1 (which is significantly higher than the average in Vietnam). In addition, countless bunkers and other structures were destroyed, and many weapons and ordnance items captured. The most significant aspect of these statistics was that the population of Seafloat killed three times their number of Viet Cong. This was a striking demonstration of the leverage that river power could obtain from a modest and effective commitment of men and material.

Another product of "river power" was the effect it had on the economics in the Seafloat area. An enemy document, captured in August 1969, revealed that during a previous American operation in the Lower Ca Mau Peninsula, the VC lost potential revenue because of the U.S. presence. This prohibited the VC from extorting taxes from in the villages. It is estimated that Seafloat deprived the VC of 60 million piasters, which is equivalent to almost $300,000.

Aside from the formidable psychological, tactical, and economic results of Seafloat, its impact on Vietnamization is worthy of note. Initially, the PsyOps program was a joint effort, with the U.S. Navy turning over the entire program to the Vietnamese Navy after only three months of operations. The VNN developed the area so effectively that a complete hamlet was built for the South Vietnamese government. The Vietnamese were also able to commit still more tactical forces—two PCFs and ten yabuta junks.

A new shore base, called Solid Anchor, is presently being built, and will be turned over to the Vietnamese Navy later this year. When this has been done, the VNN will then have complete tactical responsibility in addition to the PsyOps program.

Perhaps the most important aspect of Seafloat is the potential of this type of power projection in future limited wars. To this end, the formidable leverage available in the psychological, tactical, and economic areas should not be solely war-oriented. There are many areas of the world in which the capabilities of Seafloat could be used to pursue ecological goals. A Seafloat, for example, could be established to improve the health and sanitation of primitive areas, and this could be extended to improve literacy and to project a favorable governmental image. Essentially, it would be an inland Project Hope effort. Where possible political unrest was suspected, the government could quickly situate a Seafloat unit in those areas to project an appropriate government image.

The modest investment of men and material in Seafloat form, coupled with its inherent ease of mobility, would provide a form of warfare and "peace-fare" that would have numerous applications throughout the world. Seapower transformed into "river power" is indeed a formidable concept.

16 "Forgotten Lessons of Riverine Warfare"

Lieutenant (junior grade)
Christopher A. Abel, USCG

U.S. Naval Institute *Proceedings*
(February 1982): 64–68

A NATION'S RIVERS are its territorial arteries, carrying the lifeblood of commerce and communication to peoples and regions throughout the land. Moreover, many internal waterways tie inland areas to the sea, transforming them into major international highways. In addition, virtually all are potential natural barriers of the first order. Thus, from a military standpoint, the control of an adversary's inland waterways can be a multifaceted weapon of immense strategic importance. Indeed, history is replete with examples of the critical role which capably trained riverine forces played in time of war. Yet despite its undeniable significance, the doctrine of riverine warfare has traditionally been neglected by the United States. As a consequence, American soldiers and sailors have consistently been forced to learn and relearn the more or less timeless lessons of riverine combat under the press of battle. While these tragic trial-and-error episodes of the past cannot be undone, they certainly need not be repeated in the future.

Put simply, riverine warfare consists of combat operations carried out from restricted inland waters against a surrounding countryside either wholly or partially hostile to the waterborne forces involved. As such, it entails the use of both afloat and ground elements operating in unusually close liaison and depending upon fundamentally important mutual support. The phenomenon is hardly new. In fact, the riverine heritage of the United States dates back to the Second Seminole Indian War of the 1840s. By the close of the American Civil War, some two decades later, large-scale and sophisticated riverine forces had convincingly proven their worth in the struggle to preserve the Union. Later, ad hoc versions of those same Civil War units played an important role in the turn-of-the-century battles of the Philippine Insurrection and later still in several Pacific campaigns of World War II. Nevertheless, in each instance, the riverine forces concerned labored in almost total ignorance of the lessons learned by their counterparts in past struggles. None had the benefit of implementing a time-tested and comprehensive doctrine of riverine force organization and operation. Each simply learned its specialized craft from scratch.

That the past lessons of riverine warfare had not been retained, refined, and applied to subsequent conflicts was largely a product of organizational dynamics within the American military hierarchy. To be sure, neither the Army nor the Navy was ever made wholly responsible for the prosecution of combat from inland waters. Instead, for more than 100 years, the riverine forces of the United States consisted of bastard units composed of elements from both services acting under a succession of joint command structures. As a result, neither organization was ever able to view riverine warfare as a specialty reserved for itself. Instead, both saw the phenomenon as at least partially the province of the other branch and so generally ignored it. This institutional inertia virtually guaranteed that American riverine combat expertise would never be able to survive any peacetime period.

Unfortunately, the wartime record of riverine command was also less than perfect. In fact, at one point in the early days of the Civil War, the naval commander of the Mississippi riverine forces had "come to the decision to obey no more orders issuing from Army officers."[1] On another occasion, General U.S. Grant ordered the Navy's riverine vessels into action without so much as advising their operational commander that the squadron was being used. As it was, the startled naval officer first learned of his command's participation in the undertaking when he received the after-action reports of his subordinates.[2] Yet the most convincing evidence of the weaknesses inherent in joint riverine command structures was probably that provided by the comparison of the overall effectiveness of such organizations with that of the autonomous Mississippi Marine Brigade, a specially trained and outfitted riverine combat team made up of vessels, troops, and support elements placed under a single, homogeneous command. For two years, the brigade operated against Confederate guerrillas on a number of western rivers, consistently demonstrating that its innovative single command concept was far and away the most operationally effective formula for riverine force organization in any theater. That same elemental truth was further borne out some 80 years later by the storied Dinassauts of the French Navy in Indochina. Consisting of afloat and infantry components under a single operational command, these French units successfully battled the Viet Minh for nearly a decade (1946–1954) on the Bassac and Mekong rivers of the region. Indeed, American military analysts were so taken by the notion of this "unique" force that it was heralded as being "one of the most productive developments of [that] counterinsurgency campaign."[3]

As a matter of fact, it was the end of the Dinassaut period that ushered in the most recent U.S. bout with the challenges of riverine warfare. And it was at this same point that American riverine amnesia once again took hold. Relying upon U.S. organizational manuals which simply had no provision for the kind of homogeneous riverine command represented by the Dinassauts of the French, American naval advisors quickly saw to it that the infant South Vietnamese Navy abandoned the troublesome structures in favor of more traditional river assault groups (RAGs).[4] Essentially an emasculated version of their French predecessors, the RAGs consisted solely of afloat elements without the critical presence of an organic ground force to round out the riverine equation. Moreover, the RAGs were all but officially under the operational control of a Vietnamese Army which could neither appreciate their problems nor their potential.[5] As a result, the RAGs gradually lost their combat effectiveness and ultimately yielded large segments of their Mekong Delta operating area to the control of the Viet Cong.

By late 1965, American military planners had decided that a fresh organizational approach was necessary to regain control of the Mekong Delta. Additionally, it was determined that this new undertaking should be carried out by American servicemen instead of the increasingly ineffective riverine units of the Vietnamese Navy. What resulted was the creation of Task Force 116. Code-named "Game Warden," the all-Navy force was charged with the protection of local commerce and communication on the labyrinthine waters of the region, a chore it performed admirably throughout the term of its existence. Yet Task Force 116 was simply not enough, and the reason was as simple as the solution: aggressive and successful riverine combat is carried out *from* the water and not merely on it. As such, the Game Warden units were seriously hamstrung by the absence of an organic ground force capable of carrying the battle to the enemy ashore. Thus, in the latter half of 1966, the Mobile Riverine Force was taken from the Pentagon's drawing boards and made into a reality.

In its design, the Mobile Riverine Force brought together a sophisticated assortment of established riverine hardware and concepts. Put simply, a new, assault-oriented Navy river task force would be joined to a brigade-sized body of ground troops specially trained for and dedicated to riverine operations. Both would operate as a single tactical entity, supported by highly mobile bases afloat and assisted by a limited organic air component. Such a force would at last be able to arm the most successful concepts of homogeneous riverine force structure with the latest in 20th century military technology.

Given this country's wealth of experience in river combat, the Mobile Riverine Force should have emerged as nothing less than the ultimate American riverine creation, an example of riverine organizational doctrine at its very best. Instead, the old bogeys of institutional amnesia and simple historical ignorance conspired to make the force a disappointing "next best" alternative from the outset. To begin with, the prior commitment of the Marine Corps' infantry in the I Corps region of South Vietnam meant that the attractive option of a battle-tested Navy-Marine amphibious force command structure would be abandoned in favor of still another ad hoc Army-Navy joint command arrangement. In fact, while the Mobile Riverine Force's bases were placed firmly under the operational control of the senior Army officer embarked, actual operations saw the force's afloat elements fall under Navy control and the ground troops answering to a separate Army hierarchy. Needless to say, such a structure could become dangerously strained in the heat of combat in a mobile environment.

This basic organizational dilemma of the Mobile Riverine Force is clearly borne out by former Army Major Josiah Bunting in his fictionalized account of his own experiences in Vietnam. In *The Lionheads*, Bunting points out that:

> There was some doubt, even, as to which embarked commander—the Army Brigade Commander or the Navy Task Force Commander . . . was really the senior authority. In the directive which initially prescribed command relationships theirs was to be one of "cooperation and coordination." It was a hedging, equivocal arrangement, entirely at the mercy of those assigned to the two jobs. Disagreements as to strategy and tactics were resolved by compromise, which kept all concerned quite happy, especially the VC.[6]

That the Mobile Riverine Force was largely able to overcome this fundamental flaw and acquit itself with distinction on numerous occasions is a credit to all who served with the organization. Yet, the simple fact of the matter is that such a herculean internal effort should never have been demanded from individuals already preoccupied with the deadly business of fighting a guerrilla war in a foreign land. Once again, the most elementary of riverine organizational lessons had been painfully learned from scratch.

On 25 August 1969, the Mobile Riverine Force was officially inactivated and its equipment transferred to the South Vietnamese Navy. From that day forward, this nation's institutionally unattractive expertise in riverine warfare once again began a predictable and steady decline. At present, the only active U.S. riverine resources are the men and boats of the Navy's two Special Warfare Groups. No dedicated riverine ground force or air element is assigned, and the floating units themselves are oriented mainly toward the support of commando-style SEAL raids and Game Warden-type surface patrols. In short, no trained force capable of carrying out sustained riverine operations against an enemy ashore exists today. What is more, unless the characteristic process of peacetime riverine decay can be reversed, American capabilities in the area will continue to deteriorate until the topic of riverine warfare is relegated to the realm of forgotten volumes on dusty shelves for yet another time.

The key to just such a reversal of the age-old cycle of American riverine experience lies in the assignment of the specialty to a single military organization capable of both maintaining its study in peace and single-handedly carrying out its precepts in war. The obvious choice for this particular mission is the U.S. Marine Corps. After all, no other service can begin to match the Corps' extensive level of experience in the area of combat operations carried out from the water. At the same time, the Marine Corps is more than institutionally schooled in the workings of the sort of flexible single command structure demanded in a riverine environment. The service also boasts its own air arm, a new riverine component which both the Army and the Navy have concluded is "essential to effective riverine operations."[7] Indeed, the Marine Corps already possesses virtually every basic prerequisite required of a viable riverine combat team. Only the transfer of afloat units currently under Navy command would be necessary to complete the initial organizational process.

Within the Corps, the specialty could be assigned to a minimally staffed "Riverine Warfare Command" which, in turn, would be further subdivided into a "Riverine Systems Command" and a "Riverine Combat Command." The systems command would be responsible for the continued development of specialized riverine materiel, while the combat command would be charged with the training and maintenance of a small cadre of riverine operational specialists. The latter organization would also maintain a "Riverine Assault Force" immediately ready for limited combat operations. All three of the larger commands would be skeleton structures essentially serving as institutional caretakers in peacetime, but capable of being fleshed out to whatever extent might prove necessary in time of war.

The alternative to the above proposal is an almost certain return to this country's pattern of recurrent riverine amnesia. And while such continued inaction may save money and avoid the imposition of an additional administrative burden in the short run, it can only lead to the courting of unnecessary military difficulties in the future. History has shown that riverine warfare is far too specialized a discipline to leave unnoticed until it is suddenly needed. Instead, positive institutional action must be taken and diligently pursued by the military planners of the United States. The future riverine success of this nation depends on nothing less.

Notes

1. James Hoppin, *Life of Andrew Hull Foote* (New York: Harper and Brothers, Publishers, 1874), p. 251.
2. John Dillon, "The Role of Riverine Warfare in the Civil War," *Naval War College Review*, March-April 1973, p. 68.
3. Andrew Nelson and Norman Mosher, "Proposed: A Counter-Insurgency Task Force," *Proceedings*, June 1966, p. 40.

4. Joseph Buttinger, *Vietnam: A Dragon Embattled*, Vol. II (New York: Frederick Praeger, Publishers, 1967), p. 1048.
5. R. L. Schreadley, "The Naval War in Vietnam, 1950-1970," *Proceedings*, May 1971, p. 184.
6. Josiah Bunting, *The Lionheads* (New York: George Braziller, 1972), p. 75.
7. William Fulton, *Riverine Operations* (Washington, D.C.: U.S. Government Printing Office, Department of the Army, 1973), p. 64, and S. A. Swartztrauber, "River Patrol Relearned," *Proceedings*, May 1970, p. 138.

Lieutenant (junior grade) Abel is a 1979 graduate of the Coast Guard Academy. From graduation until the summer of 1981, he served on board the USCGC *Reliance* (WTR-615) as deck watch officer and ship's communication officer. He is now commanding officer of the USCGC *Point Warde* (WPB-82368), home ported in San Juan, Puerto Rico. He is the author of two previous *Proceedings* articles, "A Breach in the Ramparts" in July 1980 and "Fish Stories" in December 1980.

INDEX

SERIES EDITOR

THOMAS J. CUTLER has been serving the U.S. Navy in various capacities for more than fifty years. The author of many articles and books, including several editions of *The Bluejacket's Manual* and *A Sailor's History of the U.S. Navy*, he is currently the director of professional publishing at the Naval Institute Press and Fleet Professor of Strategy and Policy with the Naval War College. He has received the William P. Clements Award for Excellence in Education as military teacher of the year at the U.S. Naval Academy, the Alfred Thayer Mahan Award for Naval Literature, the U.S. Maritime Literature Award, the Naval Institute Press Author of the Year Award, and the Commodore Dudley Knox Lifetime Achievement Award in Naval History.

The **Naval Institute Press** is the book-publishing arm of the U.S. Naval Institute, a private, nonprofit, membership society for sea service professionals and others who share an interest in naval and maritime affairs. Established in 1873 at the U.S. Naval Academy in Annapolis, Maryland, where its offices remain today, the Naval Institute has members worldwide.

Members of the Naval Institute support the education programs of the society and receive the influential monthly magazine *Proceedings* or the colorful bimonthly magazine *Naval History* and discounts on fine nautical prints and on ship and aircraft photos. They also have access to the transcripts of the Institute's Oral History Program and get discounted admission to any of the Institute-sponsored seminars offered around the country.

The Naval Institute's book-publishing program, begun in 1898 with basic guides to naval practices, has broadened its scope to include books of more general interest. Now the Naval Institute Press publishes about seventy titles each year, ranging from how-to books on boating and navigation to battle histories, biographies, ship and aircraft guides, and novels. Institute members receive significant discounts on the Press' more than eight hundred books in print.

Full-time students are eligible for special half-price membership rates. Life memberships are also available.

For a free catalog describing Naval Institute Press books currently available, and for further information about joining the U.S. Naval Institute, please write to:

Member Services
U.S. NAVAL INSTITUTE
291 Wood Road
Annapolis, MD 21402-5034
Telephone: (800) 233-8764
Fax: (410) 571-1703
Web address: www.usni.org